W9-BAS-586

The Pen Is In My Hand . . .

Exciting and Practical Ideas for Teaching Writing

By
James A. Lindon
and
Laura Nofsinger Raber

R & E Publishers

This book is sold with the understanding that the subject matter covered herein is of a general nature and does not constitute legal, accounting or other professional advice for any specific individual or situation. Anyone planning to take action in any of the areas that this book describes should, of course, seek professional advice from accountants, lawyers, tax and other advisers, as would be prudent and advisable under their given circumstances.

R&E Publishers
P.O. Box 2008, Saratoga, CA 95070
Tel: (408) 866-6303   Fax: (408) 866-0825

Book Design and Typesetting by elletro Productions
Book Cover by Kaye Quinn

Library of Congress Cataloging-in-Publication Data
Lindon, James A.
The Pen is in my hand-- now what? : exciting and practical ideas for teaching writing / by James A. Lindon & Laura L. Raber.
        p.   cm.
    ISBN 1-56875-048-X (soft) : $11.95
    1. English language--Composition and exercises--Study and teaching. 2. English language--Rhetoric--Study and teaching.
I. Raber, Laura L. II. Title
PE1404.L544 1993
428'.007--dc20
                                                            93-18914
                                                            CIP

Designed, typeset and totally manufactured in the
United States of America.

SPECIAL THANKS TO...

...The **Tuscarawas Valley Local School District** for supporting our effort to strengthen its writing program.

...The **Tuscarawas County Board of Education Office** for its continued support of our inservice workshops and for keeping us informed about profession-related issues and concerns.

...**Kent State University Tuscarawas Campus** for providing us with access to its computer lab.

...The **1992-93 computer lab assistants at Kent State Tusc.** who helped us maintain our sanity when the system failed.

...And finally, to **our students**—past and present—from **Tinora**, **Newcomerstown**, **Tuscarawas Valley**, and **Kent State** for working with us to make our writing program successful!

Thanks!!

Jim and Laura

PREFACE

There are numerous books on the market that advocate using process writing to teach students how to write. In fact, nearly every writing book agrees that the steps involved with process writing are prewriting, drafting, editing, and publishing, but we have found very few that describe *how* to teach it. That is how our book is different. In *The Pen Is in My Hand...* we define "process writing" in our terms, and we provide practical, easily adaptable, step-by-step guidelines on how to teach and implement the use of process writing in the classroom. We do this for creative and expository writing. We have used this material with some modifications in our junior high through college level classes. Through trial and error we have stretched and pulled the current trends of process writing into a writing program that has proven successful for us and our students. We have attempted to cover all the angles. In addition to expository and creative writing, we also explain how we handle the paper load when evaluating an entire class of compositions overnight, how we incorporate writing while studying literature, and also how we teach grammar. Furthermore, we tell how we use journals, writing folders, and writing portfolios.

So, is this just another book on process writing written by people with little or no classroom experience? Does it only spout theory and offer no practical help? Is it a writing process that only works under ideal conditions for a few teachers?

No! It's just the opposite. As classroom teachers we were tired of books like that. *The Pen Is In My Hand* ... not only reflects what we want in a writing process book but also represents our persistence with modifying many other writing process models.

However, before it became a book of easy to follow step by step explanations we tested it in our own classrooms. We found that although our teaching methods differed, we could adapt the program to suit our own unique styles.

How can *The Pen Is In My Hand...* take the mystery out of teaching process writing? Our book is divided in two sections: creative writing and expository writing. In each chapter we have listed common questions and concerns that are often posed to us by students as well as colleagues, and we have attempted to address these questions. In addition to answering questions, step-by-step guidelines for implementation have been provided. Then at the end of some chapters examples and sample activities have been included.

Some of our steps are the same for both types of writing, and to make following the steps easier we have repeated directions. This way readers do not have to search through the book to locate information that was mentioned in an earlier chapter.

Bear in mind that these suggestions are far from fool-proof. We did not just wake up one morning with solutions for our own classroom needs; the program has evolved over time. However, practical application of these ideas has brought us to this point, sharing what we have learned with others in our field.

Therefore, this book doesn't explain only process writing; it explains an entire writing program that can stand by itself or be used in conjunction with an existing program.

CONTENTS

CHAPTER ONE

Introduction

The Pen Is In My Hand... Now What? This universal problem is faced by students every time they start to write.

For years we struggled to help our students overcome this problem. By combining our ideas with suggestions of notable writing experts we devised a practical, flexible, workable writing process to help them become successful creative and expository writers.

Process Writing/Writing Process? Define, Please!

By definition, a process is a natural phenomenon marked by gradual changes that leads toward a particular result; it can also be defined as a series of actions or operations.

So, when we speak in terms of process writing, we mean just that–a series of steps that our students follow when they are writing a composition. These steps can be viewed as a variation of the steps in Graves' (1983) process approach to writing. In our program, students use the following steps when writing:

1. S.W.A.P.ping (Picking a Topic)
2. Making a List
3. Writing a Rough Draft and Revising
4. Conferencing
5. Writing a Final Copy (300-500 words)
6. Rewriting

The steps of our process integrate reading, writing, speaking, and listening skills. "The process is not meant to be a set of laws but a dynamic activity which can be changed to meet the students' needs in the years after school"(Murray 1985: 124). We feel this flexible process does exactly that.

Creative and expository writing are equally important, and both are taught through the process mentioned above. However, we always begin by teaching creative writing first.

Why Teach Creative Writing First?

Many students come into our classes thinking that expository writing is dull and boring, so we begin with creative writing to get them excited about writing.

How Do We Get Students Excited About Writing?

We give them very few rules to follow. In creative writing our students don't have to worry about all of their ideas fitting into a structured format. They are free to write what is on their minds and in their hearts in a manner that suits them. Creative writing gives students the opportunity to develop voice early in the year. Writer's voice is the ability of writers to share their emotions, opinions, struggles, and victories with the audience. Our creative writing lacks much of the rigid structure of expository writing. We stress detail, emotion, and a story line that flows smoothly together. There does not have to be all the traditional elements like a thesis, purpose, concern about audience, topic sentences in every paragraph, a required number of supporting details, a clincher for every paragraph, a specific format for the introduction and conclusion, and no minimum or maximum number of paragraphs is required. The students may have a one word paragraph if they wish. They may start in the middle of the story line and fill in the beginning later on. They don't have to have a well rounded conclusion that wraps up the story. If they want the audience to be left wondering what happened at the end, they may.

Later in the year we show them how to bridge the gap between creative and expository writing.

How Do We Define Expository Writing?

With our instruction of expository writing students follow the traditional structure suggested in many grammar books. They need to determine if the composition is going to be narration, description, informative, or argumentation.

At the same time they also have to be aware of their audience. For instance, what are the backgrounds, prior knowledge, and attitudes of the audience; and how are these similar or different to theirs?

A thesis is needed in expository writing to clearly state the controlling idea or focus of the paper.

Found in every paragraph of the body of the composition is a topic sentence, at least two sentences containing supporting detail, and a clincher sentence that restates the topic sentence.

A specific format must be followed for the introduction and the conclusion.

Finally, expository writing is quite often nonfiction, and there is usually a minimum and maximum number of paragraphs required.

If our definition doesn't differ from what can be found in a text book, what does? The process approach we take to reach the finished piece of exposition is the key to our successful program. The outline that follows is what we use as lecture notes when we explain creative and expository process writing to our students.

This outline is explained completely throughout the course of the book. It may not make much sense right now, but we feel sure it will be a valuable tool once teaching of process writing begins.

I. Picking A Creative Topic–Use S. W. A. P.ping (Share With A Purpose)
    A. S. W. A. P.ping is a technique where students, under teacher guidance, try to develop creativity and at the same time generate possible ideas for a writing assignment.
    B. S. W. A. P.ping is contrary to traditional brainstorming. With traditional brainstorming students have a topic selected and then try to find ideas to put in that story line.
    C. With S. W. A. P.ping students try to find a topic to develop into a story.
    D. Students should be shown a variety of ways to choose a creative writing topic. A different method should be used to introduce each writing assignment.
    E. In general these activities should be whole class, short term assignments, where all students work on the same assignment in class.
        1. These writing activities should only take 10–15 minutes.
        2. The students should try to be as creative as possible.
        3. When finished students read their creations aloud

   to the entire class.
   4. From this "swapping" of story ideas a longer com-
      position may develop. Students may hear a topic
      they like or they may get some new ideas for a
      different story line.
   5. They do not have to select the class topic as their
      own; however, if they want to use the class topic
      and develop it further, they may.
II.   Creative lists–Help students decide if they have a topic
      worth developing. This is the second most important
      step in the writing process.
   A.   The students make a list of ideas they might want to
        put into a composition. The list should answer the
        following questions:
        1. Who are the characters in your story?
        2. What are your characters like?
           a. age
           b. height/weight
           c. hair/eye color
           d. clothing
           e. hobbies
           f. favorite food
           g. hometown
        3. Where does your story take place?
           a. town
           b. state
           c. specific building
        4. What time does your story take place?
           a. morning, afternoon, night
           b. past, present, future
        5. What problem(s) are your characters going to face?
        6. What will they do to resolve the problem?
        7. How will the story end?
   B.   While writing the list the students should not worry
        about order or even if all the ideas are usable. They
        should just jot down the ideas as they pop into their
        heads.
   C.   Remember, not all of the items have to be used. This is
        just a starting point for the story.
        1. The list is essentially an outline of ideas to be
           considered when writing the rough draft.
        2. This step is the second most important part of the
           writing process for the following reasons:
           a. Now when students start a rough draft the list
              serves as a guide, a map, or a blueprint for their

                story.

b. The students may add things to their stories that are not on their lists.

c. The lists help keep the students focused on the composition topic by giving them a tentative beginning, middle, and end.

3. Once the list is completed the students must decide two things:

    a. Is there enough information here to develop into a strong composition?

    b. Is this topic worth developing?

4. If the answer is no, start the process over and make a new list and organize it.

5. If the answer is yes, move on to the rough draft stage.

III. **Rough Draft**

A. Quite often when it's time to write a rough draft a student will say,"I don't know how to start my story." Suggest they use the old standby opening, "Once upon a time." It sounds trite, but it gets them started and they may always change it later.

B. Using the organized list as a guide, the student now writes the rough draft quickly, all in one sitting. Writing the entire story first is more important than developing individual sections because it provides a framework upon which to build.

C. While writing the rough draft pay no attention to spelling, grammar, punctuation, or even paragraphs. Worrying about mechanics breaks the flow of the writing.

D. After the rough draft is written, the next step is to revise it. Revisions should be made right on the rough draft, because recopying the story wastes valuable time. While revising, it is important to examine the whole paper one step at a time. The following items will aid revision:

1. Use strong verbs whenever possible

2. Use vivid detail and try to create a picture with words

3. Divide the story into paragraphs

4. Check for spelling errors

5. Check for shifts in verb tense

6. Check for errors in sentence structure

7. Check for punctuation errors

IV. Conferences

   A. Conferencing and revising are closely related in that both are necessary if writing is to improve. This is the most important step in the writing process for several reasons:

      1. It offers immediate feedback from peers and the teacher in the form of constructive criticism or praise.

      2. It provides an audience for whom to write.

      3. By reading the paper aloud the students hear what they write, and if they have trouble reading it smoothly, it is probably written incorrectly.

      4. This also provides reinforcement for active listening skills as well as verbal and written communication skills.

   B. Conferencing steps

      1. Each student must complete two conferences, preferably not with friends.

      2. One student (the reader) reads his story to another (the listener).

      3. Throughout the conference the writer always retains possession of his paper.

      4. After the paper has been read to him, the listener writes up an evaluation using the teacher's guidelines.

      5. This process should take between 15 and 20 minutes.

   C. Conferencing Guidelines

      1. Was the beginning of the story interesting? Yes or No?

         a. If it was, what made it interesting?

         b. If not, why wasn't it interesting?

      2. Was there any vivid detail used in the story? Yes or No?

         a. Write the sentence that contains the best detail.

         b. Choose any sentence and add detail to it.

      3. Was there any emotion used in the story? Yes or No?

         a. Write the sentence that contains the best emotion.

         b. Choose any sentence and add emotion to it.

      4. Write a brief summary of the story based on the following elements:

         a. Who? (main character)

         b. What? (main events in the story)

      c. Why? (reasons the main events happened)

      d. When? (time)

      e. Where? (setting)

  5. Did you like the ending of the story? Yes or No?

      a. If you did, why did you like it?

      b. If you did not, what was wrong with it?

D. One half of the first conference is complete once the listener writes the evaluation.

  1. Now the students switch roles; the reader becomes the listener and the listener is now the reader.

  2. The students repeat the process of reading, writing, and evaluating.

E. Now one conference is completed.

  1. After the first conference is held, students return to their seats and review the evaluation that was written for them.

  2. The students do not have to agree with what is in the evaluation; they should, however, consider the suggestions. This should take between 5 and 10 minutes.

F. Next is the second conference. Generally the first conference takes an entire class period; therefore, the second conference takes place the following day.

  1. It is important to stress that revisions should continue even if the seven-step plan has already been completed.

  2. When students begin the second conference, they have different partners.

  3. The students repeat the entire process once again.

G. While the students conference with one another, conferences with the teacher are simultaneously held.

  1. These conferences last between 3 and 5 minutes and are not the same as the student-to-student conference.

  2. Teacher conferences are used to iron out problems that students have with their papers.

  3. These conferences also give the teacher a "feel" for the paper's content, its tone, and from whose point of view the paper is written.

H. After the conferencing is complete, the finishing touches should be made on the rough draft, and students should begin working on the final copy.

V. Final Copy–Final copies will vary in form depending on the individual teacher's preference. It is safe to assume that these recommended guidelines are generally ac-

ceptable.
A. Final copies should be written only in blue or black ink.
B. Writing should be only on one side of the paper.
C. Every paper should include a title.
D. On a separate piece of paper at the end of the composition, the students should include a paragraph that gives their opinions about their work. They should comment on the story line, the detail, the emotion, and also the flow of the story.

VI. Grading the Final Copy—As with many other aspects of teaching, grading procedures differ from teacher to teacher. Here again, some suggestions are offered. Grading for advanced and general level classes should be handled somewhat differently.
A. Because one of the underlying purposes of this writing process is to show the students success, they are awarded points for completing each step of the writing process.
B. Up to this point, students at all levels earn their points in the same way; if the steps are completed, then they receive the points.
C. Final copies for advanced classes may be rated on a holistic grading scale. General students may find a holistic scale too abstract; therefore, a percentage grade is recommended.
D. A holistic scale looks at the overall paper; it does not focus on specific areas. Students' compositions are assigned a number. The number does not correlate with a letter grade; this number merely lets the student know your overall impression of his work. The holistic scale is designed for flexibility.
E. Holistic grading scale example:
   6 = Papers that are clearly excellent. The top score of 6 is reserved for that paper clearly above a 5. The paper develops the story line with excellent detail, emotion, and insight. It also displays strong use of language and mechanics.
   5 = A thinner version of the excellent paper. It is still impressive but not as well handled in terms of detail, emotion, language, and mechanics.
   4 = An above-average paper. It has a strong story line but may be deficient in one of the essentials mentioned above.
   3 = An average paper. It maintains a general story line and shows some sense of organization but is weak

in detail, emotion, language, and mechanics.

   2 = A below average paper. It makes an attempt to deal with a story line but demonstrates serious weaknesses in detail, emotion, organization, and mechanics. It is unacceptable for most standards.

   1 = A story line that has almost no redeeming quality. It may be very brief or very long, but will be scarcely coherent and full of mechanical errors as well.

   0 = A blank paper or an unacceptable effort.

F. When evaluating creative writing, look primarily for three things: story line, emotion, and detail.

G. The holistic evaluation of each paper should be done quickly and efficiently. The grading should take between 3 and 8 minutes; this includes reading and making comments on each paper.

H. Mark no mistakes found in the text. If the errors are marked within the composition, the student does not learn to identify and correct his weaknesses.

   1 Make all comments concerning the story line, emotion, and detail at the end of the story.

   2 Also make a brief reference to other major errors that occur in the composition. However, these errors have little effect on the holistic grade.

   3 This grading method forces the student to reexamine his paper and to find and correct the errors.

I. Now the students repeat the entire writing process again. With each writing unit the students complete two compositions in a row because working on just one composition does not provide enough writing practice for each student. Students need to be aware that not every idea makes a great composition, and that's ok. Each composition is, however, a learning experience. By writing two in a row the students also have the opportunity to learn from their previous mistakes.

VII. Rewrites

A. Near the end of each quarter the students have to choose their favorite composition from that quarter and rewrite it.

B. Through rewrites students have the opportunity to further develop a final copy using the holistic grade as their guide.

C. All of the steps prior to the rewrite are actually practice steps.

   1. The final copy now becomes the rough draft.

2. The students are given one day in class to conference again. Prior to this conference students should revise their final copies.

3. Rewrites are collected approximately one week prior to the end of the grading period, and because these papers are a refined final copy, they should take very little time to grade.

4. Rewrites are graded for a letter grade. Because the students have been given ample opportunity to improve their composition, it should count as a weighted grade.

5. When grading the rewrite evaluate all aspects of writing. This includes mechanics as well as detail, emotion, and story line. Mark the mistakes in the text as they are found.

6. After the first rewrite is completed and returned to the students, they will have a more complete understanding of the writing process.

VIII. Picking An Expository Topic—Use S. W. A. P.ping (Share With A Purpose)

A. S. W. A. P.ping is a technique where students, under teacher guidance, try to develop creativity and at the same time generate possible ideas for a writing assignment.

B. S. W. A. P.ping is contrary to traditional brainstorming. With traditional brainstorming students have a topic selected and then try to find ideas to put in that story line.

C. With S. W. A. P.ping students try to find a topic to develop into a story.

D. Students should be shown a variety of ways to choose an expository writing topic. A different method should be used to introduce each writing assignment.

E. In general these activities should be whole class, short term assignments, where all students work on the same assignment in class.

1. These writing activities should only take 10–15 minutes.

2. These writing activities should allow for main ideas, supporting details, and transitions.

3. When finished students read their creations aloud to the entire class.

4. From this "swapping" of story ideas a longer composition may develop. Students may hear a topic they like or they may get some new ideas for a

different story line.

5. They do not have to select the class topic as their own; however, if they want to use the class topic and develop it further, they may.

IX. Expository lists–Help students decide if they have a topic worth developing. This is the second most important step in the writing process.

   A. The list should include the following ten items:

1. Topic
2. Purpose
3. Audience–For whom am I writing? What do I know of their background and prior knowledge–attitudes, mine and theirs?
4. Tone–attitude and word choice
5. Thesis–the controlling idea or focus of the paper. It states what you'll write about, gives the purpose of the paper, and suggests the tone.
6. Title–should tell the topic and the purpose and still sound interesting
7. Main ideas–there must be at least two. Each gets its own paragraph.
8. Supporting details–there should be at least two for each main idea.
9. Transitions–There should be one transition for each main idea.
10. Conclusion–How will you wrap up this paper?

   B. Remember, not all of the items have to be used. This is just a starting point for the story.

1. The list is essentially an outline of ideas to be considered when writing the rough draft.
2. This step is the second most important part of the writing process for the following reasons:
   a. Now when students start a rough draft the list serves as a guide, a map, or a blueprint for their story.
   b. The students may add things to their papers that are not on their lists.
   c. The lists help keep the students focused on the composition topic by giving them a tentative beginning, middle, and end.
3. Once the list is completed the students must decide two things:
   a. Is there enough information here to develop into a strong composition?
   b. Is this topic worth developing?

    4. If the answer is no, start the process over and make a new list and organize it.

    5. If the answer is yes, move on to the rough draft stage.

X.   Rough Draft

  A. Using the organized list as a guide, the students now write the rough drafts quickly, all in one sitting. Writing the entire story first is more important than developing individual sections because it provides a framework upon which to build.

  B. While writing the rough draft pay no attention to spelling, grammar, punctuation, or even paragraphs. Worrying about mechanics breaks the flow of the writing.

  C. After the rough draft is written, the next step is to revise it. Revisions should be made right on the rough draft because recopying the story wastes valuable time. While revising, it is important to examine the whole paper one step at a time. The following items will aid revision:

    1. Underline topic sentences

    2. Put parentheses around the clincher sentences

    3. Number each supporting detail–eliminate unnecessary details

    4. Circle all transitions used

    5. Check to make sure the introduction and conclusion match

    6. Check for shifts in verb tense

    7. Check for errors in sentence structure

    8. Check for punctuation and spelling errors

    9. Use strong verbs when possible

    10. Use vivid detail–try to create a picture with words

XI. Conferences

  A. Conferencing and revising are closely related in that both are necessary if writing is to improve. This is the most important step in the writing process for several reasons:

    1. It offers immediate feedback from peers and the teacher in the form of constructive criticism or praise.

    2. It provides an audience for whom to write.

    3. By reading the paper aloud the students hear what they have written, and if they have trouble reading it smoothly, it is probably written incorrectly.

    4. This also provides reinforcement for active listen-

ing skills as well as verbal and written communication skills.
B. Conferencing steps
 1. Each student must complete two conferences, preferably not with friends.
 2. One student (the reader) reads his story to another (the listener).
 3. Throughout the conference the writer always retains possession of his paper.
 4. After the paper has been read to him, the listener writes up an evaluation using the teacher's guidelines.
 5. This process should take between 15 and 20 minutes.
C. Conferencing Guidelines
 1. Did the introduction get your attention? What did the introduction tell you?
 2. Is there only one main idea in each paragraph? List the main ideas.
 3. Are there enough supporting details for each main idea?
  If yes, list the supporting details in the best paragraph.
  If no, suggest some supporting details for a paragraph.
 4. List all transitions used to connect paragraphs.
 5. What is the most important idea in the composition?
 6. Are there any technical terms used in the composition? If so, are they defined? If not, could any be added? If so, where?
 7. Does the composition end with a strong impression? If yes, what is the strong impression? If no, how could it become stronger?
D. One half of the first conference is complete once the listener writes the evaluation.
 1. Now the students switch roles; the reader becomes the listener and the listener is now the reader.
 2. The students repeat the process of reading, writing, and evaluating.
E. Now one conference is completed.
 1. After the first conference is held, students return to their seats and review the evaluations that were written for them.
 2. The students do not have to agree with what is in

the evaluation; they should, however, consider the suggestions. This should take between 5 and 10 minutes.

F. Next is the second conference. Generally the first conference takes an entire class period; therefore, the second conference takes place the following day.
   1. It is important to stress that revisions should continue even if the seven-step plan has already been completed.
   2. When students begin the second conference, they have different partners.
   3. The students repeat the entire process once again.

G. While the students conference with one another, conferences with the teacher are simultaneously held.
   1. These conferences last between 3 and 5 minutes and are not the same as the student-to-student conference.
   2. Teacher conferences are used to iron out problems that students have with their papers.
   3. These conferences also give the teacher a "feel" for the paper's content, its tone, and from whose point of view the paper is written.

H. After the conferencing is complete, the finishing touches should be made on the rough drafts, and students should begin working on the final copies.

XII. Final Copy–Final copies will vary in form depending on the individual teacher's preference. It is safe to assume that these recommended guidelines are generally acceptable.

A. Final copies should be written only in blue or black ink.

B. Writing should be only on one side of the paper.

C. Every paper should include a title.

D. On a separate piece of paper at the end of the composition, the students should include a paragraph that gives their opinions about their work. They should comment on the story line, the detail, the emotion, and also the flow of the story.

XIII. Grading the Final Copy—As with many other aspects of teaching, grading procedures differ from teacher to teacher. Here again, some suggestions are offered. Grading for advanced and general level classes should be handled somewhat differently.

A. Because one of the underlying purposes of this writing process is to show the students success, they are awarded points for completing each step of the writing process.

B. Up to this point, students at all levels earn their points in the same way; if the steps are completed, then they receive the points.

C. Final copies for advanced classes may be rated on a holistic grading scale. General students may find a holistic scale too abstract; therefore, a percentage grade is recommended.

D. A holistic scale looks at the overall paper; it does not focus on specific areas. Students' compositions are assigned a number. The number does not correlate with a letter grade; this number merely lets the student know your overall impression of his work. The holistic scale is designed for flexibility

E. Holistic grading scale example:

    6 = Papers that are clearly excellent. The top score of 6 is reserved for that paper clearly above a 5. The paper develops the story line with an interesting introduction and conclusion and supports the main ideas with strong detail. It also displays educated use of language and mechanics.

    5 = A thinner version of the excellent paper. It is still impressive, but not as well handled in terms of introduction, main ideas, supporting details, conclusion, language, and mechanics.

    4 = An above average paper. It has strong story line but may be deficient in one of the essentials mentioned above.

    3 = An average paper. It maintains a general story line and shows some sense of organization, but it is weak in its introduction, main ideas, supporting details, conclusion, language, and mechanics.

    2 = A below average paper. It maintains a general story line but demonstrates serious weaknesses in its introduction, main ideas, supporting details, conclusion, language, and mechanics. It is unacceptable for most standards.

    1 = A story line that has almost no redeeming quality. It may be brief or very long, but it will be scarcely coherent and full of mechanical errors as well.

    0 = A blank paper or an unacceptable effort.

F. When evaluating expository writing, look primarily for these things: strong introduction and conclusion, one main idea per body paragraph, supporting details, and transitions.

G. The holistic evaluation of each paper should be done quickly and efficiently. The grading should take between 3 and 8 minutes; this includes reading and making comments on each paper.

H. Mark no mistakes found in the text. If the errors are marked within the composition, the students do not learn to identify and correct their weaknesses.

1. Make all comments concerning the story line, emotion, and detail at the end of the story.

2. Also make a brief reference to other major errors that occur in the composition. However, these errors have little effect on the holistic grade.

3. This grading method forces the students to reexamine their papers and to find and correct the errors.

I. Now the students repeat the entire writing process again. With each writing unit the students complete two compositions in a row, because working on just one composition does not provide enough writing practice for each student. Students need to be aware that not every idea makes a great composition, and that's ok. Each composition is, however, a learning experience. By writing two in a row the students also have the opportunity to learn from their previous mistakes.

XIV. Rewrites

A. Near the end of each quarter the students have to choose their favorite composition from that quarter and rewrite it.

B. Through rewrites students have the opportunity to further develop a final copy using the holistic grade as their guide.

C. All of the steps prior to the rewrite are actually practice steps.

1. The final copy now becomes the rough draft.

2. The students are given one day in class to conference again. Prior to this conference students should revise their final copies.

3. Rewrites are collected approximately one week prior to the end of the grading period, and because these papers are a refined final copy, they should take very little time to grade.

4. Rewrites are graded for a letter grade. Because the

students have been given ample opportunity to improve their composition, it should count as a weighted grade.

5. When grading the rewrite evaluate all aspects of writing. This includes mechanics as well as detail, emotion, and story line. Mark the mistakes in the text as they are found.

6. After the first rewrite is completed and returned to the students, they will have a more complete understanding of the writing process.

References

Graves, D. (1983). *Writing: Teachers and Children at Work*. Exeter, New Hampshire: Heinemann.

Murray, D.M. (1985). *A Writer Teaches Writing*. Boston: Houghton Mifflin Company.

CHAPTER TWO

Who Needs Success? We All Do!

Getting our students to want to write is not always easy because many times in the past they have had bad writing experiences. So, we make them want to write by forcing them to be successful. That's right–we force them to be successful.

How Can Every Student Become a Successful Writer?

We help our students become successful by stressing the writing process and not the final product (composition). This differs greatly from the traditional way of teaching writing. The traditional method told students to brainstorm, write a rough draft, revise it, write a final copy, and only turn in the final copy. Then the final copy was dissected by the teacher and graded. The brainstorming and rough drafts were basically ignored. Plus, there was no explanation given how or why to do the steps, and no one else helped the students get ready for the final copy. No incentive like a grade or points was ever given to the students to complete anything but a final copy. As a result, a final is all many of the students ever completed.

On the other hand, we not only give our students guidelines for completing all the steps leading to a final copy but also help them revise. We reward them with points when they turn in each step of the process.

Following the steps of our process is a lot like a pianist getting ready for a recital. Very few pianists can just sit down and play a piece of music that they have never practiced. They would probably make many mistakes, and the music would lack flow and feeling. The same could probably be said about many writers who sit down and write a final copy without practice.

To avoid performing poorly, pianists practice. Their practices are broken down into drills that are repeated many times. Next these drills are put together into a whole program. Then someone listens to them and gives suggestions for improvement. Finally they are able to give their best effort to the recital.

Process writing is much the same. We give the students guidelines to follow for each step. They also get helpful suggestions from each other and us. The difference is that in addition to the incentive of putting their best effort into their final copies they receive points for completing each step leading to the final copy.

Even though the final products or performances may not be perfect, they will both improve if the same steps are followed each time according to the prescribed guidelines.

The incentive of awarding points at the completion of each step does several things. First, it removes students' fears about failure. If the students know up front that their honest efforts will be rewarded, they will be more likely to take risks with their writing. Awarding points also removes competition among students; they work to improve themselves. Another advantage is that it allows all students in the class the opportunity to earn the same number of points, no matter what their past grades have been.

Because the ultimate goal of our program is turning out independent writers, we use the point system to help ensure that independence. As stated earlier, awarding points for completing each step stresses the process and not the final product. We are convinced the product will improve by systematically repeating the steps of the process. This awarding of points keeps the students practicing because they can see some positive results.

Each step below is an example of a student's progression through the process. The steps are worth a maximum of 100 points. "When graded for completing a writing task, students need not worry specifically about their grades. Yet they still gain valuable practice with writing and come to experience its innate satisfaction" (Bechtel 1985: 166).

S.W.A.P.ping Activity–Once completed the student

receives points   (0–100)
List–The student receives points for turning in the
list   (0 -100)
Rough Draft–When the rough draft is turned in the
student receives points   (0 -100)
Conferencing–After completing two conferences
the student receives points for each of them
(0–200)
Total = (0–500)

At this point the students have had the opportunity to accumulate a maximum of 500 points, and they have not yet turned in a final product. We have forced them to be successful writers because we stress the process; the students are not permitted to move on to the next step without completing the previous one. They feel good about their work and accumulating guaranteed points. When the students feel good about what they are doing, they are willing to try even harder. Awarding points is the best motivational device we have encountered. The points are not just given away. The students must put forth enough effort to earn the 100 points for each step; they can receive any score between 0 and 100. Just because they complete each step does not ensure that they will produce a great composition. It only ensures they will be rewarded for a good effort. If both the teacher and students work together, improvement will take place in time.

This sounds pretty idealistic, doesn't it? It really isn't. The whole process simply requires classroom management for successful implementation. As soon as the tardy bell rings our students pass in their assignments, and they spend five minutes engaged in journal writing. During this five minutes we have time to take attendance; look through the lists, rough drafts, or conferences; record points; and return the students' papers. Chapter Nine discusses the role of journals in the writing process.

The next step requires the students to produce final copies. Later in the grading period, these final copies will be used to complete the final part of the writing process–the rewrite. Therefore, the final copy is not the end of the overall process; it is merely a product of it.

We do not assign a letter grade to the final copy; instead we use a holistic rating to show the students our impression of their work. Holistic scoring will be discussed in depth in chapters Ten (creative) and Twenty (expository).

Holistic scoring by itself is hard to sell to students because it is new and different. However, using it in conjunction with awarding points is not only an efficient, time saving method for evaluation but also the catalyst that makes our students want to write.

Because a holistic rating is simply our impression of the students' work, we only read through the paper, make some general comments at the end, and write a number 0-6 on it. These numbers do not represent letter grades.

Our students are not penalized for errors. Rather, we say to them through the holistic score, "Look, this is what I think of your story in terms of story line, detail, and emotion." Then, in the comments we note things like, "You have several run-on sentences and lots of spelling errors."

If students choose not to turn in a final copy, they have not completed the steps of the writing process. True, they have accumulated a large number of points by completing the preliminary steps, but without completing the final copy they are not permitted to complete a rewrite at the end of the quarter.

Very briefly, a rewrite is one of the final copies that the students have turned in during the grading period. In our classes rewrites are the only compositions that receive a letter or percentage grade. To ensure that the students take the rewrite seriously, it counts as five grades. In our grading system that equals 500 points. If students are missing a final copy and cannot complete a rewrite, they receive zero out of five hundred points for the rewrite. Suddenly, all the points that the students were awarded for completing the first four steps of the process are not very significant. At best they have 500 out of 1,000 possible points.

What's the Teacher's Role in Building a Successful Writing Program?

Students can tell right away whether or not teachers are enthusiastic about what they are teaching. Teachers must generate interest in writing and demonstrate the significance of the writing process. The students' interest can be maintained through teacher modeling. Teacher modeling is a strong selling technique because the students see the teacher doing the same writing steps they are expected to do. Some steps of the process should be modeled by the teacher every time the class writes.

For example, the teacher can S.W.A.P. every time the students do. In the early stages of implementing a writing program, the teacher's example will break the ice and encourage hesitant students to share their work.

Another time that students can see the teacher completing steps of the process is making a list. This can be done after all the students have shared their S.W.A.P.ping exercises. Try writing a list on the chalkboard based on ideas that were mentioned during S.W.A.P.ping. Make it look easy and non-threatening; show the students that it is not difficult to put together a story line.

In addition to S.W.A.P.ping and making a list, conferencing is a great way to model steps of the writing process. During conferencing, both the reader and the listener play active roles.

What Makes a Successful Writing Program?

A successful writing program is dependent on a process. A process is a set of actions, changes, or operations occurring or performed in a special order toward some result. A process that requires all students to follow all the steps of the process all the time will generate success. Process provides stability.

Another factor that determines the success of a writing program is the teacher's flexibility. This is how well the teacher adapts the process to differences in each class.

Parts of the process may not seem to run smoothly at first, but if teachers believe in the process and are persistent it will produce solid writing results. Teachers may have to make modifications in our original model to fit their own classes.

References

Bechtel, J. (1985). *Improving Writing and Learning*. Boston: Allyn and Bacon.

CHAPTER THREE

Goals

Goals are a part of everyone's life. Sometimes they are attained quickly and viewed as being too easy. Sometimes they are not attained at all and become discouraging. To avoid these two problems, we wanted our goals to be challenging yet attainable.

Each goal is realistic and attainable, but not every student will reach all the goals. Some students may only achieve one or two; however, if students follow the steps of the writing process their writing will improve in varying degrees.

Too many goals can confuse and stifle young writers. Therefore, we present our students with four long term goals. Naturally, some students reach the goals quickly then say, "Now what?" They must realize that once goals are reached, consistently maintaining them is important. It's a lot like setting the goal of becoming a millionaire. If the goal is reached but nothing is done to ensure it, eventually it may be lost. What has been gained?

What Do We Expect from Our Young Writers?

The first creative writing goal is for students to write as fluently, colorfully, and emotionally as people speak. What does this mean? Simply, we want the stories to have flow, feeling, and personality.

When given the choice of either hearing or reading about a fun-filled day at an amusement park, our students choose to hear it. Why? They say it is easier to picture.

Can students write with storytelling enthusiasm? Yes, they can, but it takes time. Learning to write, fluently, colorfully, and emotionally is a long term goal, and process writing gives students a chance to become storytellers on paper.

Using vivid detail throughout a story is goal number two. Vivid detail is painting a picture with words. Items in a story should be written as the writers picture them. This helps all readers visualize the same mental image as the writer.

For example, "It was a big house," can lead to many different pictures. However, "It was a three story white mansion with pillars in front, and black shutters on each of the thirty-seven windows," creates a common picture between writer and reader. When readers are better able to follow the writer's thought process, they can more accurately comprehend the story.

The third goal, using strong emotion, causes young writers to raise their eyebrows and put puzzled looks on their faces. They must put themselves into their writing. They must accurately portray how they would feel if they were the characters in the story. Their characters should seem realistic.

For example, "His face turned red, he clenched his teeth, his forehead wrinkled, his bloodshot eyes bulged out of his head, and he stomped out of the room," forms a clearer picture than merely writing, "He was mad at me."

Many young writers are not willing at first to put their own feelings and personalities into their stories and assume the role of each character. As a result, their stories often read like dull newspaper summaries rather than creative pieces of writing.

Developing emotion evolves slowly, and for that reason we again stress long term goals. Some writers might show improvement in expressing emotion early in the year, while others might take all year before they grasp even a small portion.

Goal four, becoming a writer and thinking as a writer, is the most difficult goal to sell students. To them writers are people who write novels, short stories, or poetry, not high school students.

Generally, the high school students have just not written enough to even remotely consider themselves writers. After using the writing process all year, our students have made the following comments: "I can do a better job of stream of consciousness than Katherine Anne Porter"; "Sometimes that Hemingway guy got a little long on his detail"; "Boy, Steinbeck sure paints a good picture with words."

At this point we know our students are aware of writing and are learning to discern, not only what they like to read, but also why they like it.

When Do We Set the Goals for Our Students?

Before we give the goals of our writing program to our students, we begin with a broad discussion about goals. Generally, many of our students have participated in some type of organized activity (Boy Scouts, Girl Scouts, athletic teams, church groups) where they had the opportunity to set goals, and we allow the discussion to progress from there.

After the initial question (What are some of the goals that your group set for itself?) we look at the scope of the goals. For the most part, the goals are something to aim for over a period of time, and that is when we make the connection to writing.

We tell the students that process writing is a long term change; some students may see improvement in their writing skills immediately while others may see no real change until much later in the school year. By following the steps of a process, students' writing will improve, but all students won't progress at the same rate.

Once the goals of a group have been discussed, we switch gears and talk about personal goals. This is when students seem to grasp the purpose of the discussion. Nearly every one of us has set goals that we haven't been able to attain for one reason or another. By moving the discussion from general to personal, the students tend to take ownership in the four goals that we've set for them.

Do the Students Always Understand the Goals?

Students who do not seem to relate to the meaning of the writing goals may need gentle prodding. Perhaps they don't understand vivid detail or what writing fluently, colorfully, and emotionally means. Flood them with examples. For instance, write the following sentences on the chalkboard:

1.   "Ouch," Dan said. "I dropped a brick on my toe."

2.   I knew my mom was really mad.

Ask them if sentence one is a realistic representation of how Dan would have reacted when he dropped the brick on his toe. Again, tell them to picture the scene in their heads, and ask them some leading questions like "What do people do when they drop something heavy on their foot?" Hopefully, they will respond with answers such as "They pull their foot back in pain; they take their shoe off to examine the damage; they hop up and down on one foot." Those are realistic responses.

The second example about the angry mom should be fairly simple for the students to relate to. Ask them how they can tell when their moms are mad. Again, we expect responses like "She grits her teeth; the veins in her neck pop out; her eyes bulge; her face turns red; smoke seems to roll out of her ears; she calls me by my full name." These, too, are realistic answers.

Stressing that attaining goals is a long term process will be a major help when students feel they are not seeing immediate results.

CHAPTER FOUR

Creative
S.W.A.P.ping

"Few writers are lucky enough to have an inspired, full-blown idea and supporting details spring into their minds in a beautifully complete and organized manner" (Parker 1991: 208). We never assign writing topics to our students. To help them choose a topic to develop into a paper they use S.W.A.P.ping. S.W.A.P.ping is an acronym for Sharing With A Purpose.

S.W.A.P.ping is contrary to traditional brainstorming. With traditional brainstorming students have a topic selected and then try to find ideas to put in that story line; however, with S.W.A.P.ping, students try to find a topic to develop into a story.

A creative S.W.A.P. is used to stimulate creative thinking and is less structured than an expository S.W.A.P.ping activity which has main ideas, supporting details, and transitions built-in. Students should be shown a variety of ways to choose a writing topic and a different method should be used to introduce each writing assignment.

How Does S.W.A.P.ping Work?

In general, S.W.A.P.ping activities should be whole class, short term assignments, where all students work on the same assignment in class. These writing activities should only take ten to fifteen minutes, and the students should try to be as creative as possible. When they are finished, the students read their creations aloud to the entire class. From this "swapping" of story ideas a longer composition may develop. Perhaps students may hear a topic they like, or they may get some new ideas for a different story line. The students do not have to select the class topic as their own; however, if they want to use the class topic and develop it further, they may.

Why Should the Teacher S.W.A.P.?

Teacher modeling is important throughout the process, and the teachers should share their paragraphs and suggest some topics they could write about. The teacher's participation also builds confidence in the process for both the teachers and the students. Both are learning the process together, and both are writers searching for topics.

What Does a Creative S.W.A.P. Involve?

Any directed writing can be a creative S.W.A.P.ping activity. Several sample S.W.A.P.s appear at the end of this chapter.

This first explanation incorporates a creative S.W.A.P.ping activity with "how to" suggestions. Begin by putting the entire class in a circle, so they can all see each other. Next, show them a stuffed teddy bear. Then, ask them to write the following questions:

1. What is the bear's first, middle, and last name?
2. Who is its owner?
3. Where does the bear live?
4. What are the bear's hobbies?
5. Why does the bear crave red popsicles?
6. How did the bear hurt its paw?
7. Where does the bear want to go for vacation?
8. Why does the bear's owner neglect it?

Now give the class ten minutes to freely express themselves by writing a creative paragraph that answers all of the questions. Next comes the sharing. When finished, students are expected to read their creative efforts aloud to the entire class. From the sharing the students are searching for story ideas. The following examples show how the students can benefit from collaborating to choose their writing topics: (1) A student reveals that the bear hang glides as a hobby; another student decides to write a story about a hang glider in California, (2) Someone tells that the bear craves red popsicles because he has recently had its tonsils removed; someone else decides to write about a mad scientist who performs experiments on innocent animals, (3) It is revealed that the bear hurt its paw in a surfing accident while vacationing in Hawaii; upon hearing this, a student decides to write about a hula dancer who falls in love with a hippie surfer.

If the students do not find a topic of their own after the first S.W.A.P., don't worry. Suggest they further develop the S.W.A.P.ping exercise. After a while students usually generate their own topics. This builds individual ownership into their writing because it now becomes "my topic" and "my story" rather than "the topic I was assigned."

S.W.A.P.ping offers unlimited possibilities for story ideas; the students are limited only by their own imaginations.

How Much Time Is Spent S.W.A.P.ping?

S.W.A.P.ping generally takes one to two days to complete depending on the size of the class. The first day is needed to get it started, and the next day should wrap it up. The second day can then be used to make their lists.

References

Parker, J.F. (1991). *Writing Process to Product.* Evanston, Illinois: McDougal, Littell & Company.

Creative Writing S.W.A.P.ping Activity
"G.I. Blues"

Find a picture of a soldier and show it to the class. Ask them to briefly answer the following questions in a short paragraph. When the students have finished writing, have them share their creations aloud.

1. What is the soldier's name?

2. What is he thinking?

3. Where is he going?

4. What is his favorite color?

5. Why does his left foot itch?

6. What did he do before he entered the army?

7. What is his family like?

Creative Writing S.W.A.P.ping Activity
"If You Only Knew What I Do"

Pass a teddy bear around the classroom. After each student has had a chance to examine it, ask them to briefly answer the following questions in paragraph form. When the students are finished writing, have them share their creations aloud.

1. Who owned this bear?

2. What secrets did it share with its owner?

3. What is the bear's full name?

4. When did the owner get the bear?

5. Where is the bear's favorite place to be?

6. Why are the bear and its owner separated?

Creative Writing S.W.A.P.ping Activity
Setting

Find a picture of the interior of a house and show it to the class. After they have had a few minutes to study the picture, ask them to answer the questions below in a brief paragraph. When the students have finished writing, have them share their creations aloud.

1. List five words to describe this room.

2. What kind of story might take place in this room?

3. Without using the name (red, blue, etc.) how could you describe the colors in this room?

4. Describe the size of this room.

5. Describe the furnishings in the room.

6. What sounds might you hear in this room?

7. How does this room smell?

Creative Writing S.W.A.P.ping Activity
"Oh, the Places I've Been"

Put a pair of shoes in front of the class where everyone can view them. Ask them to look carefully at the shoes and then answer the following questions in a brief paragraph. When the students have finished writing, have them share their creations aloud.

1. Who do these shoes belong to?

2. Where are some of the exciting places that these shoes have been?

3. Describe these shoes.

4. Why doesn't the owner want these shoes any longer?

5. What would these shoes say if they could talk?

VARIATION: Use various shoes to get the students to think from a different perspective. For example, if the pair of shoes are children's size, the students might think from a child's point of view. Or if the shoes are ladies' dress shoes, the students might tell a different story than if you had chosen combat boots.

VARIATION: With an older group of students you may wish to throw in some "off the wall" questions to help generate even more ideas for a story. In addition to the above questions, you could include the following:

6. Why doesn't the owner like the Smith's French Poodle?
7. How/when did the owner originally acquire these shoes?
8. What was the worst experience these shoes ever had?
9. Describe an ideal day for these shoes.

Creative Writing S.W.A.P.ping Activity

"On the Road Again"

Read the following scenario aloud to the students; then select one of the writing activities for the students to complete:

You are a semi with an absent-minded driver. Even though he is so scatterbrained, you like your driver a lot. One afternoon while you are stopped to refuel, your driver wanders away and becomes lost. You and the local police search for hours but are unable to locate your driver.

DETAIL

The police force artist wants to sketch a picture of your driver so that they can put out a missing person report. Describe your driver as well as you can. Include name, hair/eye color, age, height, weight, physical build, clothing, and anything else that may be useful to the police department.

EMOTION

Write a brief paragraph explaining how you felt when you realized that your driver was really lost.

SUCCINCTNESS

You decide to place an ad in the newspaper's Lost and Found Column. You search your entire cab (ashtray, under the mats, between the seat cushions) and only come up with ten dollars in change and three dried up pieces of gum. The ad will cost fifty cents per word, so you have to choose your words carefully.

Creative Writing S.W.A.P.ping Activity
"Color My World"

Read the following information to your students and ask them to respond to the questions that follow:

Chameleons are lizards that have the ability to rapidly change the color of their skin in order to blend in with their surroundings. In addition to this special talent, their eyes move independently of each other which allows them to look forward and backward at the same time. If you were given these unusual abilities, how would you use them?

1. Where would you slither first? Once there, what color would you become?

2. How could looking in different directions be advantageous?

3. Imagine that you crawled into your favorite fast food joint. What color would you change to?

4. You become brave and venture into the room of your best friend. S/he is talking on the telephone, and you eavesdrop on the conversation. Suddenly you realize that you are the topic of the conversation. What do you find out?

CHAPTER FIVE

Creative Lists

We feel making the list is the second most important step in the writing process, and flexibility and structure are important components for it to work effectively.

People make lists every day, from shopping for groceries and homework, to checking the space shuttle for lift off. So the next step of our process requires the students to make a list of ideas to include in the composition. The list serves as an outline for the story, and rough drafts will flow better and more easily if the students have made detailed lists.

What Should Be on a Creative List?

Stress that they are trying to paint a picture of their stories with their words. The list should contain answers to the following seven questions:

1. Who are the characters in your story?
2. What are your characters like?
   a. age
   b. height/weight
   c. hair/eye color
   d. clothing
   e. hobbies
   f. favorite food
   g. hometown
3. Where does your story take place?
   a. town
   b. state

     c. specific building

4. What time does your story take place?

     a. morning, afternoon, night

     b. past, present, future

5. What problem(s) are your characters going to face?

6. What will they do to resolve the problem?

7. How will the story end?

The following example shows how easy it is for a creative list to evolve:

1. Names–John J. Smith and Bridgett S. Jones
2. Physical description–John–5'6", 340 lbs., red hair, green eyes, even when dressed in a three piece blue suit, John looks like a hobo, hobbies include hang-gliding and bowling, his favorite food is shrimp and pizza, and he is from Cleveland.

     Bridgett–6'4", 111 lbs., 27, blond, blue eyes, blue jeans, Harley Davidson t-shirt, a face only a mother could love, hobbies include playing Bingo and reading romance novels, she enjoys all greasy fried foods, and is from Akron.

3. Setting–An old rickety, sun bleached, red barn in Darby, Montana, fifteen miles from nowhere.
4. Time–It is midnight on a cool summer evening. The ground is wet from the dew, and the sky is clear. The full moon is illuminating the barnyard, and the stars are polluting the sky.
5. John and Bridgett meet at the barn to watch the meteorite shower. John is an astronomer, and Bridgett is his assistant. The squeaking legs on the telescope stand are driving John crazy. He tells Bridgett to go into the barn to look for an oil can. Bridgett returns with an oil can, but when she turns it upside down a sleepy genie tumbles out.
6. They talk to the genie who agrees to grant each of them one wish.
7. John wants to be a famous scientist; Bridgett wants to be a model.

While writing the list the students should not worry about order or even if all the ideas are usable. They should just jot down the ideas as they pop into their heads.

Not all the items in the list have to be used. Items may also be added to the list later, if the students wish. The list is just a

Not all the items in the list have to be used. Items may also be added to the list later, if the students wish. The list is just a starting point for the story. Essentially it is an outline of ideas to be considered when writing the rough draft.

This step is the second most important part of the writing process because now the students have a guide, map, or blueprint for their story. They also have a tentative beginning, middle, and end to work with.

What Purpose Does a List Serve?

Once the list is completed and organized the writers can see for themselves if there is enough information for a composition of 300 to 500 words in length. If they feel there is enough information, they move on to the next step, the rough draft.

If there isn't enough information, they pick a new topic and start a new list. Before they write a whole story, the list lets the students know if they have enough ideas worth turning into a 300-500 word composition. It is a lot easier to scrap a one page list than it is to scrap a two to four page rough draft.

Requiring the students to follow the steps each time they write emphasizes the writing process not the product (composition).

We strongly suggest that when students move on to the rough draft they should not go back and change their topic and start over. Students need to realize that not all ideas make good stories. However, they will learn to manipulate language, regardless of the story line if they follow all the steps of the process.

Creative List Form

1. Who are the characters in your story?
2. What are your characters like?
   a. age
   b. height/weight
   c. hair/eye color
   d. clothing
   e. hobbies
   f. favorite food
   g. hometown
3. Where does your story take place?
   a. town
   b. state
   c. specific building
4. What time does your story take place?
   a. morning, afternoon, night
   b. past, present, future
5. What problem(s) are your characters going to face?
6. What will they do to resolve the problem?
7. How will the story end?

CHAPTER SIX

Creative Rough Drafts and Revisions

Quite often when it's time to write a rough draft students will say, "I don't know how to start my story."

Rather than have the students just sit and look at a blank sheet of paper suggest they start, "Once upon a time." It sounds trite, but it gets them started, and they may always change it later. Most students will change the opening, but it is perfectly acceptable to keep "Once upon a time."

Another way to assist students who need help getting started is to direct them to go back to their lists. Essentially, the lists are the skeletons for their stories. Suggest they picture in their heads how the stories are going to begin; then tell them to capture what they "see" with words.

To further illustrate this, refer to the sample list in the previous chapter. The characters are John and Bridgett, and they are going to meet at an old barn. It is midnight, and the moon is full. The writer has determined all of this prior to beginning the story but now is having difficulty starting the story. Tell the student to approach the list from various angles.

Take the setting for example. Guide the students with questions like "Could you begin by describing the night and the surroundings?" or "Can you explain why John and Bridgett are at the old barn?"

Still another way that the writer could approach the story's beginning is from the perspective of a character. Perhaps the student could begin the story through a character's thoughts. For example, "A clear, cool summer night," Bridgett thought to herself, "how romantic! John and I have worked together for eight months and four days, but this is the first time he's asked me to work in such a remote place."

A final suggestion for aiding students who have trouble starting their stories is to encourage them to practice writing various beginnings in their journals. Tell them to choose an old list and start writing about it. For instance, the students could choose an item from the sample list and write about number two, the physical description of Bridgett. In a short period of time they should be able to produce several sentences that capture how Bridgett looks. "Squinting her clear blue eyes to adjust to the darkness that enveloped her, Bridgett searched the heavy blackness for John. Finding herself alone, she began to panic. Beads of sweat formed on her brow, and her blond hair hung in damp ringlets at the nape of her neck. A native of Akron and quite familiar with big city life, this 6'4" lab assistant knew she had little to fear from her deserted surroundings. Still, however, the knot in her stomach told her that something was not right; maybe it was just the greasy burger smothered with onions that she'd eaten on the way or perhaps it was the eerie glow created by the full moon. In any event, Bridgett wished that John would show up–and soon."

The more students practice, the easier and more fluent their ideas will evolve.

How Should Students Write Their Rough Drafts?

Using the organized list as a guide, the students now write their entire rough drafts quickly and in one sitting. The point of this is to get the ideas down before they are forgotten. Writing the whole story first is more important than developing individual sections because it provides a framework upon which to build.

While writing their rough drafts urge the students to disregard spelling, grammar, punctuation, topic sentences, and even paragraph rules. Arthur Daigon (1982) maintains burdening writers with finding and correcting errors only retards the flow of language onto paper. Once the rough drafts are completed, they can go back and fix the mechanics.

How Should Students Revise Their Rough Drafts?

After the rough drafts are written, they must be revised. When the students wrote the drafts they were primarily concerned with just getting down the ideas; now they need to go back to develop individual parts of the stories. Changes should be made right on the rough drafts because recopying the stories wastes valuable time. While revising, it is important to examine the whole paper one step at a time.

In order to examine rough drafts with consistency, students need to be given a simple check list to aid revision. This check list does not have to be followed in order, and the students find many of the steps have to be repeated before a final copy is ready. The following items are included in our check list:

1. **Use strong verbs whenever possible.** What is a strong verb? A strong verb can create emotion and evoke a reader's response to the story. For instance, a student may have written in the rough draft, "He got up out of the chair and went out the door."

Upon reviewing the verbs in that sentence, the student might realize "got" and "went" are weak and wimpy and they lack action, umph, and life. He might then decide to write, "He sprang from the musty grey chair and bolted out the screen door." Sprang and bolted imply that he was in a hurry and thus creates a stronger, more vivid picture for the reader. Not every verb in a rough draft needs to be changed just for the sake of changing it. However, every verb should be at least reviewed.

An extensive list of strong verbs is located at the end of this chapter.

2. **Use vivid detail and try to create a picture with words.** The writers' goal is to create in their readers' minds the same images that they "see." Getting students to write what they mean is not an easy task. Consequently, they produce sentences like "Our neighbors have a big dog." Since we all have our own interpretation of what a "big dog" is, it is important to stress to the students that they need to make their readers "see" the same dog that they do.

Guiding the students through directed writing activities will aid them in learning to visualize what they want to say before they actually write it. This can be accomplished several ways. For example, the students can use similes and metaphors to show comparisons (Our neighbors' dog is as big as my six year old brother). Also, they can address specific characteristics of the object that they are describing (The dog's paws are bigger than baseballs).

The following directed writing activity is broken down to show how to help students visualize what they want to say. Additional directed writing activities appear at the end of this chapter.

This activity can last one or more class periods depending on the class size.

First: Place a stuffed animal where all of the students can see it. For the sake of this example, the animal is a brown teddy bear.

Next: Give the students a series of questions to answer about the animal. The questions should appeal to the five senses.
1. What color is the bear's fur?
   a. What does the color remind you of?
   b. Compare the color to something else (The bear is brown like _____).
2. Describe the bear's features.
   a. What shape are the bear's eyes?
   b. What color are they?
   c. Do the eyes remind you of anything?
   d. What is its nose like?
   e. Describe its mouth.
   f. Compare the nose and mouth to something.
   g. Does the bear have any peculiar features?
3. How does the bear smell?
   a. What makes it smell this way?
   b. Compare the odor to something.
4. How does the bear's fur feel?
   a. Describe the texture of the fur.
   b. What does the fur feel like?
   c. What else feels like the bear's fur?
5. Describe the bear's feelings.
   a. What does the bear think at night?
   b. What goes through its mind during the day?
   c. Where is the bear's favorite place to be?
   d. Why does it like to be there?
6. How big is the bear?
   a. Describe it with specific comparisons.
      * How big are its paws?
      * How big are its ears?
   b. How much does the bear weigh?

    c. Compare the whole bear to the size of another object.

Now ask the students to write a paragraph about the bear that incorporates the information from the questions. A typical response might be like the one below:

"Teddy's wooly fleece reminds me of oreo cookies. His world is seen through glossy black button eyes the size of a dime, and he breathes in the fresh country air with his fuzzy pink nose. When Teddy is in his favorite place, on top of the patchwork quilt on my bed, his yarn mouth curls up in a smile. Teddy likes to relax on my bed because he catches all the gossip. Though he is no bigger than a basketball, he keeps watch over me at night and makes sure that I'm safe. During the day time Teddy admires himself in the mirror on my chest of drawers while he waits on me to return home from school. He thinks his best feature is the silky lavender bow around his neck. It smells musty, just like Teddy. Teddy retains the musty odor because he was packed away in my grandma's basement for so long."

When the students are finished writing, encourage them to share their paragraphs aloud with the class.

Over-doing detail is natural when students first begin writing. They tend to clump all the details together at the beginning of a paragraph. This is alright because too much detail is easier to work with than no detail no all.

Ideally, detail should be suggestive not blatant. Perhaps a student writes "Jim is a large man. He is 6'3" tall and weighs 185 pounds." At least this is a starting point; the reader has an idea of Jim's size. However, if it is not necessary to know his exact height and weight, the detail appears rather elementary.

This is where the teacher can step in and guide the student. Obviously the student has a picture of a big man in mind. Now ask the student to describe how tall six feet three inches is.

For example, full-grown stalks of corn are taller than 6'3" so maybe the student could incorporate that vision into the story. Instead of "Jim is six feet three inches" suggest something like "As Jim disappeared into the corn field his head could no longer be seen above the stalks" or "Jim's large frame was dwarfed by the 6'5" corn stalks."

The following example demonstrates how students can be shown to sprinkle their details rather than clump them all together:

    1. Use the questions from the creative list guide.
    Question One: Who are the characters in your story?
    Question Two: What are your characters like?

       a. age
       b. height/weight
       c. hair/eye color
       d. clothing
       e. hobbies
       f. favorite food
       g. hometown

2. Have students jot down responses to these questions.

Question One: Lucinda Jones

Question Two:

       a. 7 years old
       b. 4'2"–48 lbs.
       c. light brown/blue
       d. likes jeans and baggy shirts
       e. playing football
       f. macaroni and cheese
       g. Jamestown

3. Now ask the students to write a paragraph that describes the character they have created.

Initially, responses might be similar to this:

"Lucinda Jones is seven years old. She is 4'2" and weighs forty-eight pounds. Lucinda has light brown hair and blue eyes, and she likes to wear blue jeans and baggy shirts. She also likes to play football and to eat macaroni and cheese. She lives in Jamestown."

This is an example of detail overkill. The student has lumped every detail into six sentences.

4. Once the students have written a paragraph about their character, ask them to turn it into more of a description. Encourage them to spread out their detail, to imply it where possible.

"My best friend is Lucinda Jones. Her nickname is Cindy, but I call her LuLu. LuLu is a tomboy, probably because she's the only seven year old girl in Jamestown. Her favorite clothes are jeans and baggy shirts which is good because we play football nearly every afternoon. Even though LuLu is only 4'2" and weighs less than fifty pounds, she can out play most of us boys. When we finish playing, my mom usually invites LuLu to stay for lunch. Lu's light brown curls bob up and down as she agrees to stay, and her blue eyes light up when Mom says we're eating macaroni and cheese, LuLu's favorite."

From the above example, the reader gets a strong picture of LuLu through the eyes of another character, and even though there is not one word mentioned about the narrator the reader gets a good picture of him, too.

These exercises can be completed for all parts of the creative list before the students actually write a story.

The third and fourth questions from the list deal with a story's setting.

> Question Three: Where does your story take place:
>   a. town
>   b. state
>   c. specific building/room
> Question Four: What time does your story take place?
>   a. morning, afternoon, night
>   b. past, present, future

Students could practice setting up a story before they actually begin writing the plot.

The remaining three questions from the creative list all have to do with the plot.

> Question Five: What problem(s) are your characters going to face?
> Question Six: What will they do to resolve the problem?
> Question Seven: How will the story end?

Roughly speaking, the answers to these questions make up the story's beginning, middle, and ending.

At the onset, dividing a list into several separate exercises rather than assigning a whole story will help the students feel more comfortable about writing. It will also allow the teacher to focus on specific sections of a story.

3. **Divide the story into paragraphs.** How can students tell when to start a new paragraph? We suggest that they start a new paragraph every time they change speakers, every time they change ideas or topics, and every time they change scenes. The following "paragraph" serves as an example:

The house seemed still and peaceful—almost too quiet. Amanda decided to check on things before she retired for the evening. Slowly, she crept to the stairs and listened. "Nothing is stirring up in the kids' rooms. That's good," she thought out loud. Next, she moved to the basement stairs. The steady hum from the furnace blower and the damp musty smell assured her that everything down stairs was as it should be. Just as she was about to turn out the kitchen light, a loud crash shattered the stillness. Amanda nearly jumped out of her skin! She raced toward the door leading to the garage. As she stood there with her heart beat pounding in her ears, she tried to muster enough courage to open the door. "O.K. On the count of three," she thought to herself. "Three-and-a-half, four...come on..." With a violent jerk on the brass knob, the door flew open. Suddenly, something charged through the opening and brushed against her. Overcome with fright, Amanda gasped loudly and passed out on the cold tile floor. She woke to find a hairy face staring intently at her. Amanda was now face to face with the cause of her anxiety. The tiny tiger striped kitten apologetically licked Amanda's cheek with its rough pale pink tongue.

Using the above guidelines it is easy to divide this into separate paragraphs.

PARAGRAPH ONE SETS UP THE STORY

The house seemed still and peaceful–almost too quiet. Amanda decided to check on things before she retired for the evening.

PARAGRAPH TWO HAS A CHANGE IN SCENES

Slowly, she crept to the stairs and listened. All was quiet. "Nothing is stirring up in the kids' rooms. That's good," she thought out loud.

PARAGRAPH THREE ALSO CHANGES SCENES

Next, she moved to the basement stairs. The steady hum from the furnace blower and the damp musty smell assured her that everything down stairs was as it should be.

PARAGRAPH FOUR HAS AN IDEA CHANGE

Just as she was about to turn out the kitchen light, a loud crash shattered the stillness. Amanda nearly jumped out of her skin! She raced toward the door leading to the garage. As she stood there with her heart beat pounding in her ears, she tried to muster enough courage to open the door. "O.K. On the count of three," she thought to herself. "Three-and-a-half, four...come on..." With a violent jerk on the brass knob, the door flew open.

PARAGRAPH FIVE ALSO CHANGES IDEAS

Suddenly, something charged through the opening and brushed against her. Overcome with fright, Amanda gasped loudly and passed out on the cold tile floor.

PARAGRAPH SIX CHANGES SCENES

She woke to find a hairy face staring intently at her. Amanda was now face to face with the cause of her anxiety. The tiny tiger striped kitten apologetically licked Amanda's cheek with its rough pale pink tongue.

With creative writing we also don't worry too much about topic sentences, supporting details, or clinchers; that is covered when we teach expository writing. Not every paragraph written in a creative story needs a topic sentence, three supporting details, or a clincher. Sometimes in longer paragraphs these parts are needed to help tie ideas together and to prevent rambling. But overall, if students worry too much about each paragraph and what it must contain, they may lose their creative ideas as well as their individuality.

4. **Check for spelling errors.** Spelling errors should not be ignored. We encourage all of our students to use dictionaries every time they write.

5. **Check for shifts in verb tense.** Verb tense is difficult, and some students may never understand it. Nevertheless it needs to be taught. Generally, students tend to have more difficulty with the present perfect and past perfect tenses than with any of the others. In addition to teaching a grammar lesson about verb tense we provide them with a few guidelines to use when checking their papers for tense errors. Those guidelines appear below:

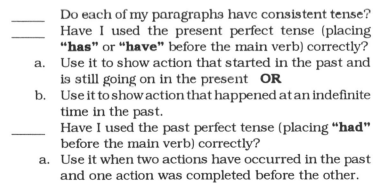

_____ Do each of my paragraphs have consistent tense?

_____ Have I used the present perfect tense (placing **"has"** or **"have"** before the main verb) correctly?

    a. Use it to show action that started in the past and is still going on in the present **OR**

    b. Use it to show action that happened at an indefinite time in the past.

_____ Have I used the past perfect tense (placing **"had"** before the main verb) correctly?

    a. Use it when two actions have occurred in the past and one action was completed before the other.

In Chapter Twelve we use verb tense to explain how students' papers are used to teach grammar.

6. **Check for punctuation errors.** We remind our students to have end punctuation marks, to punctuate conversation correctly and to make some use of commas. If they have any questions, they should always use the grammar books as a reference.

As we mentioned earlier in the chapter these revision steps do not have to be followed in this order. They may also have to be followed more than once. We realize there aren't many revision steps. However, we feel that there are enough to do an effective job of writing.

References

Daigon, A. (1982). "Toward Righting Writing." *Phi Delta Kappa.* December, 242-246.

Abbreviated Rough Draft Revision Checklist

_____1.   Use strong verbs whenever possible.

_____2.   Use vivid detail and try to create a picture with words.

_____3.   Divide the story into paragraphs.

_____4.   Check for spelling errors.

_____5.   Check for shifts in verb tense.

_____6.   Check for punctuation errors.

Rough Draft Revision Checklist

1. Use strong verbs whenever possible.

_____ Have I replaced weak verbs with strong action verbs wherever I could?

2. Use vivid detail and try to create a picture with words.

_____ Are my explanations clear?

_____ Have I created on paper the same images that I see in my mind?

3. Divide the story into paragraphs.

_____ Have I started new paragraphs when they are needed?

a. When there is a new speaker

b. When the scene changes

c. When a new idea or topic is introduced

4. Check for spelling errors.

_____ Have I looked up in a dictionary words that I'm uncertain about?

_____ Have I used **their/there/they're**, to/too/two, and **your/you're** correctly?

5. Check for shifts in verb tense.

_____ Do each of my paragraphs have consistent tense?

_____ Have I used the present perfect tense (placing **"has"** or **"have"** before the main verb) correctly?

a. Use it to show action that started in the past and is still going on in the present **OR**
b. Use it to show action that happened at an indefinite time in the past.

_____ Have I used the past perfect tense (placing **"had"** before the main verb) correctly?

a. Use it when two actions have occurred in the past and one action was completed before the other.

6. Check for punctuation errors.

_____ Do I have punctuation marks at the ends of all my sentences?

_____ Are my commas in the right places?

_____ Have I used quotation marks correctly?

Vivid Detail Exercise

The sentences below are all vague. Read the sentences, and rewrite them using vivid detail. Picture the sentence in your head and capture the image with words.

1. The dog is mean.

2. I knew my mom was mad.

3. Dad yelled when he hit his thumb with the hammer.

4. The dress is pretty.

5. The beautiful flower was growing in the garden.

6. The little kitten is mean.

7. An elephant is a large animal.

8. The house is very big.

9. Our grass is really high.

10. Her new ring is very nice.

Vivid Detail Exercise

Make a list of vivid details to describe the items below. An example has been done for you.

Wet spider webs in the morning

a. delicate, handmade crystal lace
b. handfuls of scattered diamonds
c. dewy, clinging strands
d. sparkling
e. glistening traps just waiting for unsuspecting prey

1. The setting sun on a pond

    a.

    b,

    c.

    d.

    e.

2. Leaves changing colors

    a.

    b.

    c.

    d.

    e.

3. A new dollar bill

    a.

    b.

    c.

d.

e.

4. The sun reflecting off of a person's hair

a.

b.

c.

d.

e.

5. Water rushing over rocks

a.

b.

c.

d.

e.

Strong Image Exercise

The phrases below can produce strong images. Under each phrase list as many words or phrases that you can think of to create those strong images. One has been done as an example.

frying bacon

a. sizzling   d. crackling
b. popping   e. steaming
c. splattering   f. crunchy

1. a beautiful ring

    a.   d.

    b.   e.

    c.   f.

2. a soft teddy bear

    a.   d.

    b.   e.

    c.   f.

3. a country road

    a.   d.

    b.   e.

    c.   f.

4. a pretty dress

    a.   d.

    b.   e.

    c.   f.

5. a cute puppy

    a.   d.

    b.   e.

    c.   f.

Strong Verbs

abbreviate
accent
accept
act
add
agree
allow
alphabetize
alter
analyze
answer
apply
arch
argue
arrange
articulate
ask
assemble
attend
balk
bang
bat
beat
begin
bend
bisect
bite
blend
blink
blow
bob
boomerang
boot
bounce
bound
bow
box
brush
brush
buff
build
bump
buy

calculate
calibrate
can
capitalize
carry
carve
cast
categorize
change
chart
chase
check
chew
choose
chuck
chum
circle
cite
clap
clash
clasp
classify
climb
clutch
coast
collect
collide
color
combine
communicate
compare
compile
complete
compliment
compose
compute
conduct
connect
consider
contrast
contribute
convert

cooperate
copy
correct
count
cree
cringe
crinkle
criticize
cross
crumble
crunch
crush
cut
dab
dally
dance
dart
dawdle
decrease
deduce
defend
define
delay
demonstrate
derive
describe
design
designate
detect
develop
devour
diagram
differentiate
digattempt
dine
dip
direct
disagree
discover
discriminate
discuss
display

dissect	flutter	hurdle
distinguish	fly	hurl
distribute	fold	hyphenate
dive	fold	illustrate
divide	follow	include
document	forgive	increase
dodge	form	indent
dot	formulate	indicate
double	frame	infer
drag	fray	inform
dray	gallop	insert
drift	gather	integrate
drill	generalize	interact
drink	generate	interpolate
drive	get	invite
droop	give	isolate
drop	glide	itemize
drunk	gnash	jab
duplicate	gnaw	jerk
eat	goad	jiggle
edit	gobble	jimmy
emit	gorge	jog
enter	grab	join
erase	graph	jostle
estimate	grasp	jump
excuse	grate	keep
exit	graze	kick
extend	greet	knead
extrapolate	grind	knock
fag	group	label
falter	grow	labor
feed	hammer	laugh
find	handle	launch
finger	harmonize	lead
finish	haul	leap
fire	heat	leave
fit	heave	lengthen
fix	help	lift
flap	hike	list
flee	hit	locate
flick	hoist	loiter
flinch	hold	look
fling	hop	lurch
flip	hover	make
float	hum	manipulate

map
march
mark
match
me
meander
measure
meet
melt
mend
miss
mix
modify
mold
mount
move
multiply
mute
nail
name
nip
note
number
offer
omit
operate
order
organize
outline
pace
paint
pantomime
parade
paraphrase
participate
pass
past
pat
perform
permit
pinch
pitch
pivot
place
plan

plant
plot
pluck
plunge
point
poke
polish
position
pound
pour
practice
praise
prance
predict
prepare
present
press
proceed
prod
produce
pronounce
propose
prove
provide
pry
pucker
pull
punch
punctuate
push
put
quake
quaver
question
quiver
quote
raise
ram
ramble
rap
react
read
rearrange
rebound
recall

recite
recoil
reconstruct
record
reduce
reel
regroup
relate
reorder
reorganize
repeat
replace
report
reproduce
reset
respond
restate
retell
return
revolve
rewrite
riddle
roam
rock
roll
roll
romp
rove
rub
rub
run
rush
sag
sand
save
saw
say
scamper
scour
scram
scrape
scrub
sculpt
scurry
scuttle

select
send
serve
set
sew
shake
shake
share
sharpen
shiver
shoot
shorten
shove
shrink
shrivel
shut
sign
signify
simplify
sing
sip
sit
skate
sketch
ski
skip
slacken
slide
sling
slip
slither
slump
smile
smile
smite
smooth
soar
sock
somersault
sort
speak
specify
spell
spring
sprinkle

square
squeeze
squint
stagger
stammer
stamp
stand
start
state
step
stick
stir
store
straighten
strain
stray
stretch
strike
strike
strive
stroll
struggle
subtract
suggest
summarize
supply
support
sway
swerve
swim
swing
swirl
switch
swivel
syllabic
system
tabulate
tack
take
tally
tarry
tear
tell
thank
throb

throw
time
toddle
toil
toss
tow
trace
transfer
translate
tread
tremble
trip
trudge
tuck
tug
tumble
tweak
twirl
twitch
underline
use
varnish
vault
verbalize
verify
wander
watch
wave
weigh
wheel
whirl
whisper
whistle
wiggle
wince
wink
wipe
wither
wobble
work
wrap
wriggle
wrinkle
write
yank

CHAPTER SEVEN

Creative Conferencing

Once the initial revisions are made students are ready to conference. Conferencing encourages revision because during conferencing students are seeking ways to further improve their papers.

Conferencing is time that is set aside in class for students to share their papers aloud on a one-to-one basis. Two types of conferencing simultaneously take place: student-to student and student-to-teacher.

Conferencing usually requires two days because the students must complete two student-to-student conferences in addition to one with the teacher.

Each student-to-student conference is worth up to 100 points; therefore, the students can earn a maximum of 200 points for the student conferences.

Why Is Conferencing Important?

Conferencing is the most important step of the writing process for the following reasons:
1. Students can gain many ideas for improvement through conferencing with their peers and the teacher.
2. It provides students with an audience for whom to write.

3. It offers feedback to the writers in the form of two student-written evaluations as well as verbal feedback from the teacher.
4. Students are given the opportunity to hear what they have written.
5. It uses all the language arts skills.

"Research on peer editing supports the practice. Weeks and White (1982) studied 4th and 6th graders and concluded that peer editing groups showed more improvement in mechanics and in the overall fluency of writing than the control group whose work was always teacher edited. Woodman (1975) showed that peer editing results in improved writing and editing skills. There is even some evidence that peer editing improves reading comprehension (Haley-James, 1981). You can have your students do peer editing with confidence that writing skills will improve" (Harp 1988: 830).

Why Conference?

Writers need an audience, and conferencing provides one. The writers now have the opportunity to write for someone besides the teacher. An audience offers reaction and can provide helpful insight to the writers before the story is completed. This helps writers with the task of revising their papers because writers know their stories so well that when they proofread them silently, the stories say exactly what is in the writers' minds and not necessarily what is on the paper. If the writers have trouble reading the rough drafts aloud, then the papers are probably not written smoothly.

What Adjustments Are Needed in the Classroom?

While conferencing, students take an active role in classroom management. Students now assume the responsibility for moving their desks into pairs facing each other, monitoring the volume of their individual conferences, and helping each other improve their papers by following the teacher's prescribed conferencing format and writing evaluations. The teachers do not directly control the individual conferences because they too are engaged in conferencing with students.

What Is the Prescribed Conferencing Format?

The conferencing format questions address the important elements of the composition that the teachers will look for when they grade it. The questions are designed so they cannot be answered with a yes or a no.

The following format addresses story line, emotion, and detail:

1. Was the beginning of the story interesting? Yes or No?
    a. If it was, what made it interesting?
    b. If not, why wasn't it interesting?
2. Was there any vivid detail used in the story? Yes or No?
    a. Write the sentence that contains the best detail.
    b. Choose any sentence and add detail to it.
3. Was there any emotion used in the story? Yes or No?
    a. Write the sentence that contains the best emotion.
    b. Choose any sentence and add emotion to it.
4. Write a brief summary of the story based on the following elements:
    a. Who? (main character)
    b. What? (main events in the story)
    c. Why? (reasons the main events happened)
    d. When? (time)
    e. Where? (setting)
5. Did you like the ending of the story? Yes or No?
    a. If you did, why did you like it?
    b. If you did not, what was wrong with it?

What Does Student-to-Student Conferencing Involve?

As mentioned earlier, conferencing requires two days, and the same procedure is followed on both days. During conferencing the students work in pairs. One student (the writer/reader) reads the story to the other (the listener). Throughout the conference the writer/reader always retains possession of the paper, because "the writer knows the history of the draft, knows the unseen decisions that do not appear on the page, and is the person best able to comment on the draft, stating what works and what needs work"

(Murray 1985: 150). Once the paper has been read, the listener writes up an evaluation using the teacher's conferencing format. It is possible that the reader might have to read the paper more than one time so the listener can better answer the questions.

After the listener writes up an evaluation, one half of the first conference is finished. Now the students switch roles; the reader becomes the listener and the listener is now the reader. They repeat the process of reading, writing, and evaluating.

Now one conference is completed. The reader takes the evaluation that was written and looks it over. It is the reader's responsibility to make sure the evaluation is complete because each well-written conference is worth 100 points.

The writer does not have to agree with what was written, just make sure that it was written correctly. If the reader thinks the evaluation is incomplete, it is the reader's responsibility to get a better explanation from the listener.

The written conferences may be taken from the room to further help the writers revise their rough drafts before the next day's conference.

The written evaluations must be turned in with the final copy in order for the writer to receive his 200 points. Conferences may be handed in for a grade before final copies are due. If this is done, they must still be included with the final copy. Getting the conferences early allows the teacher to spend all the grading time on the paper.

While the students conference with each other, conferences with the teacher are simultaneously held. These conferences last between three and five minutes and are not the same as the student-to-student conferences.

What Are Student-to-Teacher Conferences?

Teacher conferences are used to iron out problems that students are having with their papers. During student-to-teacher conferences the students have to offer information about their work so that the teachers can learn about the paper's content, support the students' ideas, and help out when necessary (Hansen 1992). We have found that teachers do not have to ask the same questions that are asked during the student-to-student conferences. We use a variety of conference techniques. In some conferences we ask our students to briefly summarize their stories. Sometimes we ask them to read a section of their story that has good detail or emotion. Other times we will ask them to read us their opening or ending. Still other times we will just ask them if they have any questions for us about their papers.

From the student-to-teacher conference, the teacher becomes familiar with the paper's basic content, so while evaluating the paper, the teacher is free to concentrate on the aspects of the composition that the teacher feels are important.

After the conferencing is completed, the finishing touches should be made on the rough draft, and the students should begin working on the final copy.

References

Hansen, J. (1992). "Literacy Portfolios Emerge." *The Reading Teacher*. April, 604-607.

Harp, B. (1988). "When the Principal Asks." *The Reading Teacher*. April, 828-830.

Murray, D. (1985). *A Writer Teaches Writing*. Boston: Houghton Mifflin Company.

Creative Conference Form

Title of Story_____

Writer_____ Conferrer_____

1. Was the beginning of the story interesting? Yes or No

   a. If it was, what made it interesting?

   b. If not, why wasn't it interesting?

2. Was there any vivid detail used in the story? Yes or No

   a. Write the sentence that contains the best detail.

   b. Choose any sentence and add detail to it.

3. Was there any emotion used in the story? Yes or No

   a. Write the sentence that contains the best emotion.

   b. Choose any sentence and add emotion to it.

4. Write a brief summary of the story based on the following elements:

   a. Who?   (main character)

   b. What?   (main events in the story)

   c. Why?   (reasons the main events happened)

   d. When?   (time)

   e. Where?   (setting)

5. Did you like the ending of the story? Yes or No

   a. If you did, why did you like it?

   b. If you did not, what was wrong with it?

CHAPTER EIGHT

Creative Final Copies

A final copy is not the end product of the writing process. Rather, it is a revised rough draft that is turned in as a required step of the process.

Like the other segments of the writing process, guidelines for writing a final copy must be established. Four things are required for final copies in our classes:

1. They must have a title.
2. They must be written in blue or black ink.
3. The writing can only be on one side of the paper.
4. Students must attach an opinion paragraph to the back of their compositions. The paragraph should tell how the student feels about the paper in terms of story line, detail, emotion, and flow of the overall paper.

The students, in addition to their final copy and opinion, must hand in their rough drafts, two conferences, and lists. These papers are all stapled together in the following order:

1. Final Copy
2. Opinion
3. Rough Draft
4. List
5. Two Conferences

Final copies are rated holistically rather than given a letter grade, and they are used as yet another form of feedback to the students. Holistically evaluating final copies is fully explained in Chapter Ten.

CHAPTER NINE

Journals

What Are Our Students' Journals Like?

Our students' journals are just considered practice writing. But it is different than the practicing involved with producing a final copy. Journals serve as practice for the students on their own. Our students are responsible for writing a journal entry for each day that school is in session, even if they are absent. We give them some guidelines and a time frame, and then they choose how they use journals.

The structure and time frame we give them are that each journal entry must have the following:

1. At the top of the page the date, the time the entry started, and a title
2. Five minutes of effort on anything they want to write about, but they are not to be disgusting, abusive, or offensive with what they write
3. At the bottom of the entry, the time they stopped

In addition to the entry the students must make a table of contents for the entries. In the table of contents they simply make two columns. The first column has the dates of the entries and the second column has the titles of the entries. The following is a brief example:

DATE	TITLE
9/4	"A Hot Day"
9/5	"Tired"
9/6	"My Job"
9/7	"Boy Did I Luck Out"
9/8	"The Big Game"
9/11	"Nothing to Write About"

What Do the Students Write in Their Journals?

"... Teachers who have students writing in their journals have them do so frequently. And it is this frequency which contributes to the problem of choosing appropriate content for journal writing" (Simmons 1989: 70).

We solve the problem of content by not telling them what to write. Our students choose their own topics. Journals "can be the place to discover thoughts and feelings not yet expressed. You can capture the present or recapture the past in the journal. You can explore what could be, or should be, or might have been, as well as what is. You can react to books, political events, friends, or philosophy–telling what you like or don't like about them all" (Schwartz 1985: 7).

What If Students Truly Can't Think of Anything to Write About?

Until they get a brain storm for a writing topic, we tell them to write the following sentence over and over for the next five minutes: "I can't think of anything to write today."

Quite often after the sentence is written a few times the students get a brain storm and write something else. On other occasions we have had students write this sentence over and over again for five minutes. However, because of its boring nature this kind of entry does not appear very often during a grading period. No matter what they choose to work on they are just practicing on their own. This practice might help their writing improve, because they are deciding for themselves what to work on, rather than being told what to do.

Again we can compare the students' journal writings to pianists practicing on their own. The pianists do not always practice with an instructor listening to everything they play. Most of the time they must practice on their own. The pianists know what they need work on, and while practicing on their own they can concentrate on their weaknesses. They also can take this practice time and play what they like for their own personal enjoyment. They can experiment and learn to manipulate music.

The same can be said about young writers. During journal time they can work on adding detail or emotion to their writing, or they can experiment with new words or ideas. Journals are to get the students to use the language and say what they mean.

When Do Our Students Write in Their Journals?

The first five minutes of every class is spent writing in the journals. The students begin writing as soon as the tardy bell rings. By beginning each class with journal writing, we establish a daily routine; the students know what to do without being told to do it. Also, it gives the students five minutes to unwind. Wiener (1981: 260) says, "To be effective, journal writing should probably begin soon after classes begin, when students are at their most reticent."

Why Do Students Write at the Beginning of Class?

Having journal writing at the start of each class accomplishes several things for the teachers. First, the students know when the bell rings they have a responsibility, and the teachers do not have to give them instructions every day to start class. Second, during this time teachers can take attendance and get organized for that day's lesson. Third and probably most importantly, the teachers during this time can check the lists and rough drafts that the students have due. Checking the lists and rough drafts during this time prevents the students from having down time or a time when they have nothing to work on because the teachers have their papers when they need them.

So during journal time both the students and teachers are working quietly. With a little luck and practice the teachers and students finish at about the same time and can move on the next assignment together.

Our students write in their journals every day, even when we are covering literature. If students are absent, they are expected to make the entry up outside of class.

At the end of each quarterly grading period our students hand in their journals for a percentage grade. But before we collect them we ask them to place the table of contents on top and circle on the table of contents one entry they want us to read. We also explain that the circled entry is the only one we will read. We are just going to check to see that the table of contents matches up with the number of entries and that each entry has five minutes of effort.

We determine what five minutes of effort is based on the individual student. We all know what our students are capable of. For some, five minutes of effort may only be five sentences; for others it may be half a page. Not all students are at the same level, and we take that into consideration when we check for five minutes of effort.

If the students have an entry for each day school was in session and five minutes of effort, they receive one hundred points. Those one hundred points are then recorded three times. So simply by taking five minutes out of each day and keeping their journals organized the students have earned three hundred points.

This fits into our process writing way of thinking by rewarding the students for effort. Quality and quantity are not of utmost importance. Effort is the key to success. Again we are giving our students a chance to be successful without placing them in a threatening situation.

The students need to save each group of quarterly journals until the end of the year because then they have a journal project to work on.

What Is a Journal Project?

Three weeks before the end of the school year the journal project begins. At this time the students gather up all four quarters of journals. Then we assign them a day of the week. For instance John will be assigned Monday, Joe will be given Tuesday, Mary will get Wednesday, Tom will receive Thursday, and Julie will be given Friday. This format of assigning a day will be followed until all the students in the class have a day of the week assigned to them.

Once the students have their day of the week, they next must circle on all their table of contents that corresponding date and title.

Next they make the following chart that has these headings at the top of the page:

DATE	TITLE	MOOD	A word, phrase or clause to summarize entry

The date is the day of the week assigned, for example Monday. The title is the title of each Monday entry. The mood means what mood was expressed in that entry. In the last column without revealing major content, summarize each Monday entry in a word, phrase or a clause.

The following is a brief sample chart:

DATE	TITLE	MOOD	A word, phrase or clause to
9/1	"Hot"	grouchy	88 degrees
9/8	"Test"	confident	aced a math test
9/15	"Job"	scared	started my new job
9/22	"Relatives"	disgusted	aunts
9/29	"Football"	happy	we won
10/6	"Pay Check"	happy	from here to there

We usually give the students one day to circle their day on the table of contents, put together the charts, and hand them in.

So now journals and a small amount of effort have provided students with 300 points each quarter and 200 more points at the end of the year. This totals 1400 points just based on effort.

Just because the chart is completed does not mean that the journal project is over. Now the students have one week to write a 300-500 word composition about their year based on the journal chart. They may use all or part of their chart to help them. When this composition is handed in to be graded it must also include a rough draft.

We give the students a percentage grade for this project. Now we realize it is the end of the year, and this might seem like a lot of work, but it really isn't. When we grade the projects we primarily just look for how well the students expressed themselves and told a story. Many of the compositions are entertaining and reflect real writing skills.

We do not mark any mistakes. We are truly looking for the overall flow of the story lines. The grades we assign are determined with that in mind. The scores could range between 0-100. What ever score we give, we record it five times for a maximum total of 500 points for the composition about their year.

This journal project adds finality to journals. Yes, journals are practice, but they are now more than that and are still non-threatening to the students. Donald Murray refers to his journal/writing log as a "daybook." Of it, he says, "The daybook is where I play. It is fun. It's where I fool around, noodle, connect and disconnect, doodle. I do not strain, force. I accept, receive"(1985: 70). Also, he explains that he goes back through his daybooks and picks out things that he needs to work on.

Journals and the journal project are a way of getting students to review their year and look at themselves to see how they may have changed during its course.

References

Murray, Donald M. (1985). *A Writer Teaches Writing*. Boston: Houghton Mifflin Company.

Schwartz, Mimi. (1985). *Writing for Many Roles*. New Jersey: Boynton/Cook Publishers, Inc.

Simmons, John S. (1989). "Thematic Units: A Context for Journal Writing." *English Journal*. January, 70-72.

Wiener, Harvey S. (1981). *The Writing Room*. New York: Oxford University Press.

CHAPTER TEN

Creative
Holistic Scoring

In an earlier section we discussed making the students successful by awarding points in conjunction with holistic scoring. Now it is time to look at what holistic scoring is and how easy it is to use.

What Is Holistic Evaluation?

"With this method the evaluator is not concerned about specific traits in the writing or about particular criteria (though subconsciously the teacher may very well be working from an implicit primary trait checklist based on his or her own particular biases)" (Bechtel 1985: 171).

Harvey Wiener (1981) says holistic scoring is an important approach to evaluating written works. The holistic scoring of creative final copies provides the students with immediate feedback about their work before it is turned in as a rewrite. It affords students the opportunity to focus on creating a strong composition they can revise later. Holistic scores have no bearing on the students' grades. It is not an "A," "B," "C," "D," or "F." It is just a general impression.

Holistic scales are designed for flexibility. Developing a scale that reflects individual teacher preferences is fairly easy to do. Our scale is a 0-6 rating scale, and it contains (in somewhat loose terms) our explanations of what we look for in students' papers. An example of our scale appears below:

6 = Papers that are clearly excellent. The top score of 6 is reserved for that paper clearly above a 5. The paper develops the story line with excellent detail, emotion, and insight. It also displays strong use of language and mechanics.

5 = A thinner version of the excellent paper. It is still impressive, but not as well handled in terms of detail, emotion, language, and mechanics.

4 = An above-average paper. It has a strong story line but may be deficient in one of the essentials mentioned above.

3 = An average paper. It maintains a general story line and shows some sense of organization, but is weak in detail, emotion, language, and mechanics.

2 = A below average paper. It makes an attempt to deal with a story line but demonstrates serious weaknesses in detail, emotion, organization, and mechanics. It is unacceptable for most standards.

1 = A story line that has almost no redeeming quality. It may be very brief or very long, but will be scarcely coherent and full of mechanical errors as well.

0 = A blank paper or an unacceptable effort.

Each student receives a copy of this holistic grading scale at the beginning of the year. It is used to evaluate all creative final copies. After writing one or two compositions, the students acquire a "feel" for the holistic scale. To help the students acquire this feel, we read strong examples to the class on the day that papers are returned and point out why each paper received that score. We also read good segments of lower scoring papers that reflect strong detail and emotion but that are deficient in other areas such as story line and mechanics.

How Difficult Is Holistic Scoring?

The actual rating of the papers is reasonably simple and becomes easier with time. Evaluating a 300-500 word composition should only take between three and eight minutes, and that includes reading the paper and making comments about it.

How Can a Composition Be Evaluated in Three to Eight Minutes?

The teacher becomes familiar with the paper's general story line during the student-to-teacher conference. As a result, understanding the content is not cumbersome, and more time can be spent looking for strong detail and emotion.

Should the Errors Be Marked?

We don't spend precious time marking mistakes found in the text. Research reveals that most students do not pay attention to corrections teachers make on their papers (Bechtel 1985). Instead they turn right to the end to find the final grade. Also when teachers mark the errors, students never learn to identify and correct their own weaknesses. According to Judith Bechtel (1985: 171-172) "Grading harshly when errors abound is the most common policy, the easiest to legislate, and the least effective pedagogically. Premature insistence on absolute accuracy encourages plagiarism or unacknowledged help. It may also have the effect of causing students to be overly cautious, using only simple words and structures. Better is a policy which supports risk-taking and allows students to correct errors without undue punishment."

Where Do the Teachers' Comments Belong?

All of the comments regarding the students' story line, emotion, and detail should be written at the end of the story. Any grammar errors found in the story may also be noted.

Students quickly learn that the holistic score is based on their manipulation of three areas: the flow of the story line, the use of detail, and the use of emotional language. As teachers come across papers they consider 5's or 6's, they should be read to their classes. After writing one or two compositions, students have a fairly good idea of what the teacher considers a 0-6 paper.

Once students are comfortable with holistic scoring, pluses and minuses and slashes can be used to give a more specific impression without making any comments. For example, a 4+ is more desirable than a 4- even though neither has any bearing on the students' grade. Likewise, a 3+/4- does not affect the overall grade, but it shows the students that some kind of progress has been made.

Even though holistic scoring requires some adjustment by both teachers and students, it will benefit both in the long run.

References

Bechtel, J. (1985). *Improving Writing and Learning*. Boston: Allyn and Bacon.

Wiener, H. (1981). *The Writing Room*. New York: Oxford University Press.

Creative Writing Holistic Scale

6 = Papers that are clearly excellent. The top score of 6 is reserved for that paper clearly above a 5. The paper develops the story line with excellent detail, emotion, and insight. It also displays strong use of language and mechanics.

5 = A thinner version of the excellent paper. It is still impressive, but not as well handled in terms of detail, emotion, language, and mechanics.

4 = An above-average paper. It has a strong story line but may be deficient in one of the essentials mentioned above.

3 = An average paper. It maintains a general story line and shows some sense of organization, but is weak in detail, emotion, language, and mechanics.

2 = A below average paper. It makes an attempt to deal with a story line but demonstrates serious weaknesses in detail, emotion, organization, and mechanics. It is unacceptable for most standards.

1 = A story line that has almost no redeeming quality. It may be very brief or very long, but will be scarcely coherent and full of mechanical errors as well.

0 = A blank paper or an unacceptable effort.

CHAPTER ELEVEN

Writing Folders and Writing Portfolios

Writing folders play a significant role in our writing program. As our students mature as writers, they learn how to create writing portfolios using material from their writing folders. Often times, portfolios "become collections of materials that students and teachers have reworked until they are no longer representative of the student's ability–or worse yet, not even predominantly the student's effort" (Farr 1990: 103). To avoid this kind of a collection problem our students keep both writing folders and writing portfolios.

What Are Our Students' Writing Folders Like?

Very briefly, our students' writing folders are large manila folders that the students keep in file boxes in our classrooms. These folders stay in our rooms for the entire school year; the students may only take material from the folders when they are working on revisions. This ensures that all of the students have their writing material with them; it is not at home nor in their lockers. The students are free to take their writing folders and portfolios with them at the end of the school year.

Over the course of a year, our students accumulate a diverse collection of writing, and they are responsible for keeping all of their writing in the folders. This includes compositions, in-class writings, writing on literature, and even their journals. In addition, they must log every composition on a chart that is stapled to the inside cover of the manila folder. Based on the comments that are written at the end of a final copy, the students fill in their charts each time they receive an evaluated final copy or rewrite.

This chart aids students in keeping track of their compositions as well as their progress. At the end of each quarter, we check the charts to see if the students have kept track of their compositions. If they have, we award them 100 points; if they have not, they receive a zero. A section of a blank chart appears below:

Comp. #	Title	Strengths	Weakness	Errors to correct	Score

The next example is a student's chart at the end of a semester. Simply by looking at the chart, the students can tell which of their papers have strong sections, which papers have lots of errors to correct, and which papers are potential rewrite material.

Comp. #	Title	Strengths	Weaknesses	Errors to correct	Score
1	"A Year in a Week"	Strong emotion in places. Good story line	Detail weak in spots	Sent. fragments Spelling errors Verb tense	5
2	"Jeremy and the Swing"	Emotion Detail Story Line	Use of quotation marks	Dialogue Scratch outs Run-ons	6
3	"Home at Last"	Detail Good Dialogue	Inconsistent Emotion	Awkward Sentences Verb tense	5
4	"Apple Jack"	Some good detail	Lacks emotion	Awk. sentences s/v agreement spelling errors verb tense	3
Rewrite	"Jeremy"	Fixed errors with quotes	A few run-ons	---	95%A
5	"The Trunk"	Good detail	Needs dialogue to strengthen emotion. Holes in story line.	Spelling errors Verb tense	3
6	"Revenge"	Strong story line	Needs more detail and emotion	Awk. sentences Verb tense	5
7	"Charlie"	Great detail	Story line needs work. Weak emotion	Spelling	3
8	"The Warriors"	Good detail. Some Emotion	Story line is drawn out	Use of your/you're Awk. sentences	4
Rewrite	"Grandma's Trunk"	Good emotion. Dialogue improved story	Awk. sentences. Still trouble with past perfect	---	82%B

What Purpose Does the Chart in the Folder Serve?

Using the above chart as an example, we can follow this student's progress over the course of a semester.

The first paper, "A Year in a Week," has a good story line and some strong emotion in places. The student knows that he needs to work on detail and that the major errors are sentence fragments, spelling errors, and verb tense. This paper was rated as a 5.

In the second paper, "Jeremy and the Swing," the student has very strong detail, emotion, and story line. He needs to work on using quotation marks and run-on sentences. The paper is a 6 despite the grammar errors, because the student has manipulated the language well. The story line flows, and that is one of the goals of our writing program.

"Home at Last" is also a 5. The story line is fair, but the emotion is inconsistent. This paper has some run-on sentences and some trouble with verb tense. Overall, it is not a bad paper.

The fourth story, "Apple Jack," has some large holes in the story line, and the writer did not use much emotion. However, some sections of the story have strong detail. In addition to a weak story line, there are awkward sounding sentences, subject/verb agreement problems, spelling errors, and trouble with verb tense. On our holistic scale, the paper rates a 3.

These four stories were written during the first quarter, and the student had to decide which paper he would choose for his rewrite. He chose "Jeremy" and received a 95 per cent.

Since the grading period is now over, these stories are placed in the back of the writing folder, and the student begins to log his stories for the next quarter.

As the semester progresses, we begin to expect more from our student writers. What may have been a 5 at the beginning of the year could be a 3 or a 4 closer to the end of the semester. This is demonstrated with composition number seven, "Championship Charlie." The only real grammar problem is spelling, but the story line needs development and the emotion is weak. This paper rates a 3 because it was produced nearly half way into the school year.

The second rewrite of the year, "Grandma's Trunk," earned an 82 per cent. The student used the comments to improve the story, but the rewrite still contained awkward sentences and trouble with past perfect tense.

As the school year continues, the students accumulate quite an assortment of writings. Remember, in addition to their compositions, they also keep their in-class writings and their writing on literature in their writing folders. Around February, the students begin to organize writing portfolios while still maintaining their writing folders.

Why Should Students Organize Writing Portfolios?

Many colleges and businesses utilize portfolios, and we give the students as many examples as possible. Artists create portfolios to demonstrate the various media that they can manipulate; models have portfolios that they show when they audition for an interview; advertising firms put together portfolios for ad campaigns when the firm is trying to land an account.

Our students are no different from these professionals. They, too, want to be successful, so they compile unique portfolios; they are responsible for determining the organization and presentation of the material. If the students are underclassmen, their portfolios are great records of the best work they produced during a school year. If the students are graduating seniors, the portfolios are a strong indication of what these students are capable of producing when they enter college. The portfolios are also impressive tools for students to use when they have to sell themselves at college screenings or job interviews.

The students begin choosing material for their portfolios in February. They must include the following:

1. A table of contents
2. A personal vita that provides a brief autobiographical sketch, the students' history of past writing experiences, and an assessment of their progress as writers
3. Two of their best poems
4. Two of their best creative stories
5. Two of their best expository compositions
6. One composition (creative or expository) complete with each stage of the writing process
7. Two samples of writing that the students have completed on a literature assignment
8. Their research paper
9. At least five journal entries
10. Two pieces of writing that they are not satisfied with

In addition to the above writings, the students must include a section called "Other Works." In this section, the students may include any writing that is incomplete or pieces of writing that need more work. Often times students begin working on a piece of writing that they are pleased with, but then something else comes along and they never get a chance to finish it. By providing them with this outlet, they are given a chance to show off their ideas.

The students are free to put together their portfolios in any manner they choose; this allows them to personalize their portfolios. After the students have compiled their portfolios, they are turned in for a percentage grade. Since the writing samples have already been graded, the portfolios are graded on neatness and originality of organization.

How Can Students Use Portfolios in Other Academic Areas?

Once the students complete their writing portfolios, we show them how to transfer their writing portfolio skills to other areas. When their writing portfolios are returned, the students select another reason for creating a portfolio. Then, they sketch a layout and put together a final draft. The students don't actually compile the portfolio, they just plan it and determine how to organize it.

For example, Sally really enjoys cooking and is planning to pursue a career as a dietician. A requirement in her home economics class is to complete a semester-long project. Sally decides to compile a portfolio that contains recipes for the four basic food groups.

Her rough sketch might look like this:

1. Table of contents
2. Personal vita (autobiography, past cooking experience, how she sees herself as a cook, and where she sees cooking fitting into her future)
3. Dairy (recipes for breakfast, lunch, dinner—and a list of main ingredients)
4. Proteins (recipes for breakfast, lunch, dinner—and a list of main ingredients)
5. Grains (recipes for breakfast, lunch, dinner—and a list of main ingredients)
6. Fruits/Vegetables (recipes for breakfast, lunch, dinner–and a list of main ingredients)

Her final draft will be a description of how she will organize the portfolio. In other words, it will describe how the portfolio will appear and what it will contain when it is completed. Sally's final draft could be like the one below:

My cooking portfolio will be organized in a three-ring binder. It will have a table of contents at the front, a personal vita, four sections (one for each of the basic food groups), and to begin with there will be one main dish recipe for breakfast, lunch, and dinner in each section. I will calculate the nutritional value and number of calories for each recipe.

The four sections and recipes will be as follows:

DAIRY

✍ breakfast = Cheese Omelettes
main ingredients (cheese, milk, eggs)
✍ lunch = Potato Soup
main ingredients (milk, cheese, potatoes)
✍ dinner = Cheese Fondue
main ingredients (cheese, milk)

PROTEINS

✍ breakfast = Sausage and Egg Soufflé
main ingredients (milk, cheese, eggs)
✍ lunch = Curried Lentils and Rice
main ingredients (lentils, peanuts, rice)
✍ dinner = Soybean Casserole (soybeans, dried beans)

GRAINS

✍ breakfast = Cereal Bars
main ingredients (oatmeal, wheat germ, whole wheat
    flour)
✍ lunch = Tubuli
main ingredients (wheat germ, parsley)
✍ dinner = Fried Rice
main ingredients (brown and white rice, vegetables)

FRUITS/VEGETABLES

✍ breakfast= Cranberry Salad
main ingredients (cranberries, oranges, pineapple)
✍ lunch = Spinach Salad
main ingredients (spinach, mushrooms, water chestnuts)
✍ dinner = Zucchini Casserole
main ingredients (zucchini, tomatoes, onions)

The cover of the binder will sport pictures of the four basic food groups, and each recipe will be illustrated as well.

Eventually, I would like to expand this to include full-menu meals.

Writing folders and writing portfolios play a significant role in our writing program. Moving from the broader writing folders to the more specific writing portfolios, our students learn to keep track of their own progress, to sift through their material, and to organize their work into a usable format.

Reference

Farr, Roger. (1990). "Reading Trends." *Educational Leadership.* November, 103.

Writing Folder Chart

Comp. #	Title	Strengths	Weaknesses	Errors to correct	Score

CHAPTER TWELVE

Grammar

Correct grammar usage has long been considered the key to good writing. Traditionally it has been believed that knowing the grammar rules would make students good writers. However, many students never really knew how or why grammar was a key, because they never transferred the grammar lessons in their books to their own writing. We think correct grammar usage is necessary, but we have taken a nontraditional approach to teaching grammar.

When Do We Teach Grammar?

We do not even think of teaching a grammar lesson until the first two final copies have been handed in. Having students write first gives us a good sampling of what they already know about grammar usage. Then we use the most common grammar mistakes found in the first composition to help us determine which areas of grammar to cover.

Donald Murray agrees with this line of thought when he says,

> "Few composition teachers find that teaching of grammar in advance of writing does much good. For most students the principles of grammar are abstractions, meaningless until the students are in the process of using language to discover their own meaning. At that time they become meaning-

ful–pun intended–tools of thought. I've often had students who do very well in our grammar courses who cannot write well. They know the principles, but they do not know how to apply them in evolving drafts; they know the tools, but they do not know how to use them. We should know the traditions of our language, but they are best learned within the context of making writing"(1985: 239).

We use the grammar book to teach a short lesson on the day the second final copy is returned. All other times the grammar book serves as a reference book for the students.

How Do We Teach Grammar Usage?

Since we always have our students write two compositions in a row, they know that the day the second final copy is returned they are to bring their grammar books to class. We then talk about some of the most common class wide grammar errors found in these last two compositions. The following is an example of how we teach a grammar lesson:

If fifteen out of twenty-nine students in a class had problems with verb tense, we would make verb tense the first grammar lesson of the day.

To begin with all the students need to take their last two final copies from their writing folders. The chart located in their writing folders can help them find the most recent compositions.

Next we find the rules in the grammar book dealing with verb tense. We take as long as necessary to go over and discuss the application of those rules. We do not do any of the exercises in the grammar book dealing with verb tense. We have found that the students do not always transfer the correct use of verb tense in isolated exercises to the correct use of verb tense in their own writing.

After the rules have been thoroughly discussed and explained, we have the students do two things with their final copies. They circle every "have" or "has" and put a square around every "had" found in their final copies in front of them.

There is no special reason why we start this way, other than the fact that present perfect and past perfect verb tense errors are very common problems. We recommend that the circles and squares be made in pencil or a colored ink. It will contrast with the blue or black ink used in the final copy, and the errors will be easy to spot for future reference.

Once all the students have finished circling their "have's" or "has's" and squaring their "had's", we then ask for a volunteer to read a sentence using "have" or "has" or "had". At this time we remind all the students that they have a rewrite due at the end of the quarter, and this is an ideal opportunity to get extra help to correct any errors in a final copy. After this reminder volunteers usually appear.

When the volunteer has finished reading the sentence, we as a class then determine if the verb was used correctly. We quickly refer to the corresponding rule and its usage. If the word was used correctly, we explain why it was used correctly and move on to another volunteer. If the verb was used incorrectly, the class then explains why and offers suggestions for fixing it. At no time do we simply dictate right and wrong answers. The class works together to help each other.

If teachers effectively handle the class's role as helpers, the sharing becomes a nonthreatening situation. After a while students will not just randomly pick sentences, they will volunteer sentences they know are wrong. This way they can get quicker, more specific help. Or some students will even fix their own verb tense problem and then read both the wrong and right sentences to the class. At this point of the grammar lesson we can see the students making the bridge between the rules and their own writing. This is the main focus of our approach to grammar.

This sharing and helping not only helps solve individual problems with verb tense, but it also reveals for the class the students who understand verb tense. Those students who prove to be "experts on verb tense" now are sought out by others for help on future compositions. The teachers are not the only ones who can give help when there is a problem with verb tense.

By discussing both good and bad sentences, the students are learning about verb tense using their own words. They are making practical use of grammar.

We recommend only spending one or two days on the grammar lesson. No matter how we try, grammar is just not that interesting. If a class seems to grasp the grammar concept easily, we either move on to another problem area or end the grammar lesson. If the class does not seem to make the connection right away, we may only get one grammar rule covered. We may also have to come back to a rule later and study it again to refresh some minds on its correct usage.

The chart in Chapter Twenty-four shows how we work the grammar lesson into our teaching schedule.

Is Grammar Really Necessary?

The teaching of grammar usage is necessary and controversial. A host of studies and theories conclude that the teaching of rule-based, common school grammar is ineffective because students do not transfer isolated grammar drills and skill work into their writing (Hartwell 1985). Because our students use their own compositions for grammar lessons, they can more readily see the connection between correct grammar usage and their writing. Grammar and writing are not separate concepts to them. They are meshed together now for one reason: improving individual compositions.

We have personalized the need for our students to know correct grammar usage.

References

Hartwell, P. (1985). "Grammar, Grammars, and the Teaching of Grammar." *College English*. February, 105-27.

Murray, D.M. (1985). *A Writer Teaches Writing*. Boston: Houghton Mifflin Company.

CHAPTER THIRTEEN

Creative Rewrites

Near the end of each grading period the students complete the last step of the writing process—the rewrite.

What Is the Purpose of Rewrites?

Students need the opportunity to experiment with their writing, and writing several compositions before they have to turn one in for a grade gives them that chance.

Through rewrites the students have the opportunity to further develop a final copy using the holistic grade as their guide.

How Do Rewrites Evolve?

First, a due date for the rewrite must be set. One week before the end of the grading period is a fair time.

Next, set a date for a one-day in-class rewrite conference. This should be three to five days before the rewrite is due.

Then, ask the students to choose their favorite final copy from the grading period to use for their rewrite. "Writers know more about their own abilities and progress than outsiders do. Thus, they can be the prime evaluators of themselves and their work" (Hansen 1992: 604). That final copy now becomes a rough draft, and the students should begin making changes to their stories.

Most of the changes should be made prior to the day scheduled for conferencing. This way the writer has something to gain from the new feedback that the conferencing provides.

This conferencing is student-to-student, and it is only necessary to require one conference. Because the papers are not new, teacher conferences are unnecessary when dealing with rewrites. However, the teacher should be accessible to the students if they need help.

How Are Rewrites Graded?

Rewrites count as letter grades, and because the students have been given ample opportunity to improve their stories (first through the two student conferences, the teacher conference, the holistic grade, and finally through the rewrite conference) rewrites should also count as a weighted grade. A suggestion is to count the rewrite as 500 points (the same amount that the student accumulated while writing the paper for a final copy).

All of the aspects of the writing should be evaluated. This includes mechanics as well as story line, emotion, and detail. The old final copy is handed in with the rewrite, so the teacher can see the changes made by the student.

How Much Time Is Spent Grading Rewrites?

Because the teacher has already been exposed to the basic content of the paper while grading it holistically, the time spent grading the rewrite should be minimal. Mistakes should be marked in the text as they are found, but it is unnecessary to correct them.

References

Hansen, Jane. (1992). "Literacy Portfolios Emerge." *The Reading Teacher*. April, 604-607.

Compare/Contrast Chart

Different   **Alike**   **Different**

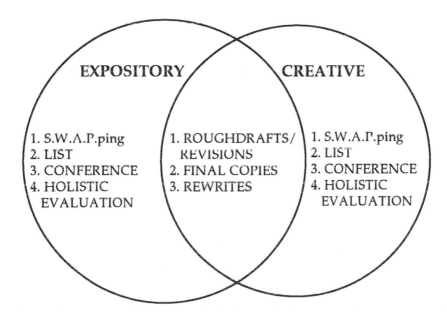

EXPOSITORY   CREATIVE

1. S.W.A.P.ping
2. LIST
3. CONFERENCE
4. HOLISTIC
   EVALUATION

1. ROUGHDRAFTS/
   REVISIONS
2. FINAL COPIES
3. REWRITES

1. S.W.A.P.ping
2. LIST
3. CONFERENCE
4. HOLISTIC
   EVALUATION

CHAPTER FOURTEEN

Linking

The chart on the previous pages shows how we link the creative and expository writing processes. The steps are the same for both, but there are some differences found within those steps. The S.W.A.P.ping activities, the information that goes into the list, the conferencing guidelines as well as the explanations found in the holistic scale vary slightly.

While the goal of creative writing is to get students to produce compositions with flowing story lines and colorful, emotional language, the goal of expository writing is to produce clear explanations. Many problems seem to arise when students begin expository writing. "The problems include students' (a) inability to sustain their thinking about topics, (b) poor organizational skills, (c) insensitivity to audience needs (e.g. not setting contexts, no use of text signals), (d) failure to provide a purpose, (e) inability to perceive themselves as informants with information to share" (Raphael 1990: 389).

Those problems are why we teach creative writing first. We feel a piece of writing may be expository and at the same time contain a creative touch. A little detail here or a little emotion there can add voice and personality to any expository writing.

Because we teach creative writing to our students first and let them become comfortable with it, they naturally use those creative techniques in expository writing. We suggest they write their compositions creatively first and not worry about topic sentences, supporting details, transitions, clinchers, introductions, or conclusions. They should get down all of their good ideas first; then they should go back and plug these good ideas into the expository format.

Below is an example of an expository composition that contains elements of creativity:

"First Impressions"

First impressions are important to a successful interview. Employers look for that little something extra in a person they want to hire.

Appearance is a key factor in considering first impressions. For example, a person wearing a cheerful smile will create an atmosphere of excitement for the available job. Another concern is to be well-groomed. Neatly combed hair, a pressed suit or dress, and freshly shined shoes will leave the possible, future employer with an impression of good personal grooming habits. Appearance is vital to a successful interview.

In addition to appearance, organization is equally important. A person should plan his day in order to be on time. Being prompt will show the company responsibility for being on time for a job. Organization also includes being prepared. Addresses and phone numbers of references should be available upon request. Asking for a phone book is not a good indication of organization or good preparation. Proof of organization creates bonus points for an interview.

Moreover, it is important to leave a lasting first impression. No person likes to be handed a dead fish handshake. A completed interview should end with a firm, strong handshake. It will express enthusiasm without saying a word. In the same way, a kind, sincere thank you will reassure that handshake. A positive lasting impression will lead to a second interview or the job.

In short, when it comes to landing a job in today's competitive market, appearance, organization, and positive lasting impressions are a must if Joe Schmoe and Jane Doe plan to be welcomed aboard the career of their choice.

The above composition contains all the elements of good expository writing. There is a strong introduction.

First impressions are important to a successful interview. Employers look for that little something extra in a person they want to hire.

It is a strong introduction because it clearly states the topic and shows that the writer is going to give the reader important information.

Every paragraph of the body has a topic sentence, at least two sentences containing supporting details, and a clincher sentence. The topic sentences are all going to be italicized. The supporting details for each are numbered. The clinchers are all in parentheses.

Appearance is a key factor in considering first impressions.

(1) For example, a person wearing a cheerful smile will create an atmosphere of excitement for the available job. (2) Another concern is to be well-groomed. Neatly combed hair, a pressed suit or dress, and freshly shined shoes will leave the possible, future employer with an impression of good personal grooming habits. (Appearance is vital to a successful interview.)

In addition to appearance, organization is equally important.

(1) A person should plan his day in order to be on time. Being prompt will show the company responsibility for being on time for a job. (2) Organization also includes being prepared. Addresses and phone numbers of references should be available upon request. Asking for a phone book is not a good indication of organization or good preparation. (Proof of organization creates bonus points for an interview.)

Moreover, it is important to leave a lasting first impression.

(1) No person likes to be handed a dead fish handshake. A completed interview should end with a firm, strong handshake. It will express enthusiasm without saying a word. (2) In the same way, a kind thank you will reassure that handshake. (A positive lasting impression will lead to a second interview or the job.)

Transitions are also used to link the main ideas. The transitions used are the following: for example, in addition to, and moreover.

A summarizing conclusion is found at the end.

In short, when it comes to landing a job in today's competitive market, appearance, organization, and positive lasting impressions are a must if Joe Schmoe and Jane Doe plan to be welcomed aboard the career of their choice.

In addition to all of these elements, there is also detail added to help the flow of the story. Some examples of detail that help the story are as follows: cheerful smile, neatly combed hair, pressed suit or dress, freshly shined shoes, dead fish handshake, and a sincere thank you. They are not much, but they make the picture a little clearer.

Emotion comes into the composition with the overall positive upbeat attitude toward the task of finding a job.

This story therefore represents a strong blend of expository and creative writing. Mixing the two does not take away from the message the students want to deliver. The mixing merely helps bring clearer descriptions and stronger emotions to the composition.

Creative writing has no specific format; however, expository writing is divided into four categories:

1. Narration
2. Description
3. Informative
4. Argumentation

Each of these serves a different need, and choosing a topic to write on depends upon the purpose of the writing.

Taffy E. Raphael found from research that enhancing students' knowledge of text structures is a key factor in teaching expository writing: "Text structures described by several researchers (e.g. Armbruster and Anderson, 1982) include comparison/contrast, problem/solution, explanation, and so forth. These different structures arise as a result of the authors' purposes. Each structure can be thought of as answering a different set of questions"(1988: 791).

We teach text structures to our students through their lists. Some of the items on the lists vary depending on which type of expository writing they are working on. If the assignment is to write a persuasive composition about a controversial subject that has three paragraphs in the body, we first provide guidance to help them establish their purpose. For example, under the "purpose" we might ask "What problem exists?" and "What is your solution?" Then, we show them how to incorporate the text structures into the paper by giving the students a question to address for each of the body paragraphs. The following is a "main idea and supporting detail" section from the list for this assignment:

Main Idea/Body
  Paragraph One: Details of the solution
    Supporting Details:
    1. What is the specific plan?
    2. What are the rules?
    3. Who will carry them out?
Main Idea/Body
  Paragraph Two: Practicality of the plan

Supporting Details:
1. Has the idea worked in other places?
2. Are any absolutes necessary to make the plan work?
3. Will the plan do what you say it will?
Main Idea/Body
Paragraph Three: Benefits of the plan for the audience
Supporting Details:
1.
2.
3.

References

Raphael, Taffy E., Becky W. Kirschner, Carol Sue Englert. (1988). "Expository Writing Program: Making Connections Between Reading and Writing." *The Reading Teacher* April, 790-795.

Raphael, Taffy E., Carol Sue Englert. (1990). "Writing and Reading: Partners in Constructing Meaning." *The Reading Teacher* February, 388-400.

CHAPTER FIFTEEN

Expository S.W.A.P.ping

To help our students choose a writing topic, we use S.W.A.P.ping (Sharing With A Purpose). Our students always choose their own writing topics.

How Does S.W.A.P.ping Work?

S.W.A.P.ping is a technique where students, under teacher guidance, try to develop creativity and at the same time generate possible ideas for a writing assignment. S.W.A.P.ping is contrary to traditional brainstorming. With traditional brainstorming, students already have a topic selected, and then they try to find ideas to put into that story line. With S.W.A.P.ping students try to find a topic to develop into a story.

Students should be shown a variety of ways to choose an expository writing topic. A different method should be used to introduce each writing assignment. In general these activities should be whole-class, short term assignments, where all students work on the same exercise in class.

Briefly, these writing activities should only take ten to fifteen minutes. Next, the S.W.A.P.ping exercises should allow for main ideas, supporting details, and transitions to develop naturally. When the students are finished with the short term assignment, they each read their creation aloud to the entire class. From this "swapping" of story ideas, a longer composition may develop. The students may hear a topic they like, or they may get some new ideas for a completely different story line. However, they do not have to select the class topic as their own, but if they want to further develop it, they may.

What Do Expository S.W.A.P.s Involve?

The following examples demonstrate how to set up an expository S.W.A.P.ping activity in a classroom:

Prompt—In life there are three things you need to know...

This prompt automatically sets up a need for an introduction, three main ideas, and a conclusion. There are numerous ways to expand any of the S.W.A.P.ping activities that are included in this book, and the variation that follows is just one example.

Variation—Show the students an antique photograph of a person, and change the prompt so it requires a narrative approach to complete the assignment. For instance, pretend this person is your great-grandmother/grandfather. S/he gave good tips about life to everyone, but the three best tips that s/he gave my mother/father were...

How Much Time Is Spent S.W.A.P.ping?

Depending on the size of the class, S.W.A.P.ping generally takes one to two days to complete. The first day is needed to get the S.W.A.P. started, and the next day should wrap it up. The second day can then be used for students to begin making their lists.

"The Bird"

Descriptive S.W.A.P.

Close your eyes and pretend you are a bird. Place yourself somewhere for five minutes. At the end of the time limit, briefly answer the list of questions in story-form. Don't forget to write an introduction and a conclusion.

1. What kind of bird are you?
2. Describe yourself.
3. Where are you?
4. What do you see?
5. What can you hear?
6. What do you smell?
7. How/what do you feel?

"The Restaurant"

Argumentative/Persuasive S.W.A.P.

You own a restaurant. Consider the following information before you begin the S.W.A.P.ping activity.

1. What kind of restaurant is it?
2. What type of clientele generally patronizes your establishment?
3. What is the average cost of a meal at your restaurant?

Give three reasons why people should eat at your restaurant. Make sure to include an introduction and a conclusion as well as supporting details for the three reasons.

"The Right Place"

Explanatory S.W.A.P.

You are going to open a series of factories. Each factory will produce one of the following products:

1. Auto Transmissions
2. Basketballs
3. Chain Saws
4. Pontoons
5. Gasoline Generators
6. Straw Hats
7. Diapers
8. Stethoscopes
9. Dynamite
10. Copper Wire

Select a factory location for at least four of the products. Explain your reasons for each location. Be specific.

"Louise's Present"

Explanatory S.W.A.P.

You own a Great Dane whose name is Louise, and for her birthday you ordered a silver mink sweater from:

Highbrow
Dept. Store
180 Way To Go
Smartie, Ohio 55555

The sweater arrived just in time for the party, and you did not have time to inspect it.

When Louise opened her gift, your excitement turned to shame, and poor Louise was broken-hearted. Not only was the sweater not silver mink (it was brown Yak), but it was for a Dachshund.

Feeling very emotional, and with a tear in your eye, write a letter to the Highbrow Department Store. Explain your feelings and also how poor Louise is in shock. Ask the department store what they intend to do to rectify the mistake.

"The Ants Are Coming"

Time Order S.W.A.P.

You are an ant. Your job is to conduct guided tours for all the important visitors. Next Thursday, a caravan of ants will arrive from the Big Hills Country. Your job is to see that they enjoy themselves while they are visiting. Here is a list of possibilities:

1. A School Kitchen
2. The Colony Dump
3. The Local Forest
4. A Syrup Factory
5. The Harbor
6. A Spa

Write a plan for a tour. List times, points of interest, potential problems, and the lunch menu. Remember that your job is to entertain and inform.

"Five, Four, Three, Two, One..."
Descriptive S.W.A.P.

Read the following information to the students and ask them to answer the questions that follow in a brief paragraph.

You are a network news anchor person. When you return from a station break, you realize that something is wrong. After a few seconds you determine that you are no longer staring into a camera; you are looking right into someone's house!

1. Describe the room that you see.
2. What do the people look like who are watching the news program?
3. What noises can you hear in the background?
4. What can you smell?

CHAPTER SIXTEEN

Expository Lists

Making a list is the second most important step in our writing program. A list helps students decide if they have enough information about the topic they have chosen, and whether or not their topic is worth developing.

What Should Be on an Expository List?

Expository lists are well-structured and keep the writing focused. The list should include the following ten items:

1. **TOPIC**–This is the broad subject of the paper.
2. **PURPOSE**–Why is this paper being written? For example, the purpose of this paper is to inform the reader about the danger of steroid use, or the purpose of this paper is to persuade the reader to vote for the upcoming school levy.
3. **AUDIENCE**–For whom am I writing? What do I know about their background and prior knowledge? How might their attitudes affect the way they perceive what I write?
4. **TONE**–What attitude should I take toward my audience? What word choice is appropriate? Do I want to be serious, sarcastic, humorous?
5. **THESIS**–This elaborates on the paper's purpose. It is a single sentence statement that tells the topic and the purpose and also suggests the tone.

6. **TITLE**–The title of an expository paper should entice the reader. At the same time, it should tell the topic and purpose of the paper and indicate the author's tone.

7. **MAIN IDEAS**–There should be a minimum of two main ideas in an expository paper. Each one has its own paragraph in the body of the paper.

8. **SUPPORTING DETAILS**–There should be at least two supporting details for each main idea. These details become the supporting sentences in the body paragraphs.

9. **TRANSITIONS**–These help the paper flow. There should be transitions at the beginning of each paragraph in the body and also before the conclusion.

10. **CONCLUSION**–How will I wrap up this paper? The conclusion should end the paper with a strong impression. It should let the reader know that the paper is finished without the benefit of "The End."

The following is an example of an expository list. In this example, assume that the assignment is to write an informative composition; also assume that the students have completed a S.W.A.P.ping activity that was geared toward informing their audience.

1. TOPIC–Writing an expository paper

2. PURPOSE–To inform the reader how easy it is to construct an expository paper.

3. AUDIENCE–High school students who don't care much for writing. Their writing experience up to now has not been overly positive.

4. TONE–Serious

5. THESIS–Writing an expository paper can be easily accomplished if the writer follows four simple steps.

6. TITLE–"Write On? Right On!"

7. MAIN IDEAS

8. SUPPORTING DETAILS

   7a. Picking a topic

      8a. What interests me?

      8b. What do I know something about?

   7b. Making a list

      8a. Include topic, purpose, audience, tone, title, thesis, main ideas, supporting details, transitions, and conclusion.

8b. Decide if there is enough information to write about this topic
7c. Writing a rough draft
    8a. Write everything down first
    8b. Revise it once everything is written
7d. Writing the final copy
    8a. Copy it in the correct form
    8b. Proofread it
9. TRANSITIONS–First, After, Once, Last, By following.
10. CONCLUSION–By following a step by step process to construct an expository paper, anyone can be successful!

What Purpose Does a List Serve?

Writing the list is the second most important part of the writing program because it essentially serves as a guide, a map, or a blueprint for the students' papers. Not all of the items have to be used, and students may add things to their compositions that are not on the list. However, this list will help students stay focused on the paper's topic.

If the students are unhappy with the information on their lists, they can make new lists before they begin the rough drafts. It is much easier to scrap a list that has taken only fifteen to twenty minutes to write than it is to write an entire rough draft before realizing that it is not going to work. If the students are pleased with their lists, they can move on to their rough drafts.

Expository List Form

1. TOPIC:

2. PURPOSE:

3. AUDIENCE:

4. TONE:

5. THESIS:

6. TITLE:

7. MAIN IDEA #1:

8. SUPPORTING DETAIL:

8. SUPPORTING DETAIL:

7. MAIN IDEA #2:

8. SUPPORTING DETAIL:

8. SUPPORTING DETAIL:

7. MAIN IDEA #3:

8. SUPPORTING DETAIL:

8. SUPPORTING DETAIL:

9. TRANSITIONS:

10. CONCLUSION:

CHAPTER SEVENTEEN

Expository Rough Drafts and Revisions

Now, using the lists as guides, the students write their rough drafts quickly, all in one sitting. Writing the entire paper first provides a framework upon which to build.

While writing the rough drafts, the students should not pay attention to mechanics. Worrying about spelling, grammar, punctuation, or even paragraphs breaks the flow of writing.

How Should Students Revise Their Rough Drafts?

Once the rough drafts are written, the next step is to revise. Encourage the students to make the revisions right on the rough drafts because recopying the whole paper wastes valuable time.

While revising, students should examine the entire paper one step at a time. The following items will aid revision:

1. Underline topic sentences. By having the students underline the topic sentence of each paragraph, they can tell right away if their supporting sentences belong in that paragraph or not.

2. Put parentheses around the clincher sentences. The clincher sentence should reflect what was stated in the topic sentence. After placing the clincher sentences in parentheses, the students can compare them to the topic sentences.

3. Number each supporting detail. Requiring the students to put numbers beside each supporting detail does two things. First, it allows the students to see whether they have enough information to support their topic sentence, and second it shows them whether or not the detail belongs in the paragraph.

4. Circle all transitions used. The transitions keep the paper flowing and need to be used between each paragraph in the body. If the students have the transitions circled, they can tell at a glance if they have used transitions or not.

5. Check introduction and conclusion. Our students can begin and end their papers in several ways. In their introductions they may ask a series of three questions, make a general statement they will support within the paper, make a startling statement to capture their audience's attention, or use an anecdote to draw in the audience. In their conclusions, they may summarize the main points of their paper, use an appropriate quotation, or end with a pertinent anecdote.

6. Check for shifts in verb tense. Verb tense is difficult and some students may never understand it. Nevertheless it needs to be taught. Generally, students have more difficulty with the present perfect and past perfect tenses than with any of the others. In addition to teaching a grammar lesson about verb tense we provide them with a few guidelines to use when checking their papers for tense errors. Those guidelines appear below:

_____ Do each of my paragraphs have consistent tense?
_____ Have I used the present perfect tense (placing **"has"** or **"have"** before the main verb) correctly?
     a.   Use it to show action that started in the past and is still going on in the present   **OR**
     b.   Use it to show action that happened at an indefinite time in the past.
_____ Have I used the past perfect tense (placing **"had"** before the main verb) correctly?
     a.   Use it when two actions have occurred in the past and one action was completed before the other.

7. Check for spelling errors. Spelling errors should not be ignored. We encourage all of our students to use dictionaries every time they write.

8. Check for punctuation errors. Students should check their papers for correct use of commas, quotation marks, and end punctuation.

9. Use strong verbs when possible. What is a strong verb? A strong verb can create emotion and evoke a reader's response to the story. For instance, a student may have written in a rough draft,"He got up out of the chair and went out the door."

Upon reviewing the verbs in that sentence, the student might realize "got" and "went" are weak and wimpy and do not say what is meant. They lack action, umph, and life. The student may decide to write, "He sprang from the musty grey chair and bolted out the screen door." Sprang and bolted imply that he was in a hurry and thus creates a stronger, more vivid picture for the reader. Not every verb in a rough draft needs to be changed just for the sake of changing it. However, every verb should be at least reviewed.

10. Use vivid detail and try to create a picture with words. The writers' goal is to create in their readers' minds the same images that they "see." Getting students to write what they mean is not an easy task. Consequently, they produce sentences like "Our neighbors have a big dog." Since we all have our own interpretation of what a "big dog" is, it is important to stress to the students that they need to make their readers "see" the same dog that they do.

The first four items on the list are specifically geared to our expository writing program. By requiring the students to underline, make parentheses, number, and circle things on their rough drafts, we can check at a glance to see whether they are following the prescribed guidelines.

Expository Rough Draft Checklist

_____1. Underline topic sentences

_____2. Put parentheses around the
clincher sentences

_____3. Number each supporting detail—
eliminate unnecessary details

_____4. Circle all transitions used

_____5. Check introduction and conclusion

_____6. Check for shifts in verb tense

_____7. Check for errors in sentence
structure

_____8. Check for punctuation and spelling
errors

_____9. Use strong verbs when possible

___10. Use vivid detail–try to create a
picture with words

Rough Draft Revision Checklist

1. Underline topic sentences

_____ Have I underlined the topic sentence in each paragraph?

2. Put parentheses around the clincher sentences

_____ Have I put parentheses around each clincher sentence?

_____ Does each clincher sentence reflect the topic sentence?

3. Number each supporting detail–eliminate unnecessary details

_____ Have I numbered the supporting details?

_____ Are there at least two supporting details for each main idea?

_____ Have I crossed out the unnecessary details?

4. Circle all transitions used

_____ Have I circled all of the transitions?

_____ Did I use a transition between each paragraph in the body of the paper?

5. Check introduction and conclusion

_____ Is my introduction acceptable?

_____ Have I used a series of three questions? **OR**

_____ Have I made a general statement that I support throughout the paper? **OR**

_____ Have I made a startling statement that will gain my audience's attention? **OR**

_____ Have I used an anecdote to draw in my audience?

_____ Is my conclusion acceptable?

_____ Have I summarized the main points of the paper? **OR**

_____ Have I used an appropriate quotation? **OR**

_____ Have I used an anecdote to summarize my main ideas?

_____ Does my conclusion repeat the ideas that I mentioned in the introduction?

6. Check for shifts in verb tense

_____ Do each of my paragraphs have consistent tense?

_____ Have I used the present perfect tense (placing **"has"** or **"have"** before the main verb) correctly?

    a. Use it to show action that started in the past and is still going on in the present

    b. Use it to show action that happened at an indefinite time in the past.

_____ Have I used the past perfect tense (placing **"had"** before the main verb) correctly?

  a. Use it when two actions have occurred in the past and one action was completed before the other.

7. Check for spelling errors

_____ Have I looked up in a dictionary words that I'm uncertain about?

_____ Have I used their/there/they're and your/you're correctly?

8. Check for punctuation errors

_____ Do I have punctuation marks at the ends of all my sentences?

_____ Are my commas in the right places?

_____ Have I used quotation marks correctly?

9. Use strong verbs when possible

_____ Have I replaced weak verbs with strong action verbs wherever I could?

10. Use vivid detail–try to create a picture with words

  Are my explanations clear?

_____ Have I created on paper the same images that I see in my mind?

CHAPTER EIGHTEEN

Expository Conferencing

Once the initial revisions are made, students are ready to conference. Conferencing encourages revisions because during conferencing students are seeking ways to further improve their papers.

Conferencing is time that is set aside in class for students to share their papers aloud on a one-to-one basis. Two types of conferencing simultaneously take place: student-to-student and student-to-teacher.

Conferencing usually requires two days because the students must complete two student-to-student conferences in addition to one with the teacher.

Each student-to-student conference is worth up to 100 points; therefore, the students can earn a maximum of 200 points for student conferences.

Why Is Conferencing Important?

Conferencing is the most important step of the process because students can gain many ideas for improvement through conferencing with their peers and the teacher; it provides students with an audience for whom to write; it offers feedback to the writers in the form of two student-written evaluations as well as verbal feedback from the teacher; students are given the opportunity to hear what they have written; it uses all the language arts skills.

Why Conference?

Writers need an audience, and conferencing provides one. The writers now have the opportunity to write for someone besides the teacher. An audience offers reaction and can provide helpful insight to the writers before the composition is completed. This helps writers with the ongoing task of revising their papers.

Writers know their compositions so well that when they proofread them silently, the papers say exactly what is in the writers' minds and not necessarily what is on the paper. If the writers have trouble reading the rough drafts aloud, then the papers are probably not written smoothly.

What Adjustments Are Needed in Classroom Management?

While conferencing, students take an active role in classroom management. Students now assume the responsibility for moving their desks into pairs facing each other, monitoring the volume of their individual conferences, and helping each other improve their papers by following the teacher's prescribed conferencing format and writing evaluations. The teachers do not directly control the individual conferences because they, too, are engaged in conferences with students.

What Is the Prescribed Conferencing Format?

The conferencing format questions address the important elements of the composition that the teachers will look for when they grade it. The questions are designed so that they cannot be answered with a yes or a no.

The following format addresses what we look for in our students' expository compositions:

1. Did the introduction get your attention?
   What did the introduction tell you?
2. Is there only one main idea in each paragraph?
   List the main ideas.
3. Are there enough supporting details for each main idea?
   If yes, list the supporting details in the best paragraph.
   If no, suggest some supporting details for a paragraph.

4. List all transitions used to connect paragraphs.
5. What is the most important idea in the composition?
6. Are there any technical terms used in the composition?
   If so, are they defined?
   If not, could any be added? If so, where?
7. Does the composition end with a strong impression? If yes, what is the strong impression?
   If no, how could it become stronger?

What Does Student-to-Student Conferencing Involve?

As mentioned earlier, conferencing requires two days, and the same procedure is followed on both days. During conferencing the students work in pairs. One student (the writer/reader) reads the story to the other (the listener). Throughout the conference the writer/reader always retains possession of the paper. However, in order for the listeners to correctly answer questions two and three they have to see the text. Once the paper has been read, the listener writes up an evaluation using the teacher's conferencing format. It is possible that the reader might have to read the paper more than one time, so the listener can better answer the questions.

After the listener writes up an evaluation, one half of the first conference is finished. Now the students switch roles; the reader becomes the listener and the listener is now the reader. They repeat the process of reading, writing, and evaluating.

Now one conference is completed. The reader takes the evaluation that was written and looks it over. It is the reader's responsibility to make sure the evaluation is complete because each well-written conference is worth 100 points.

The writer does not have to agree with what was written, just make sure that it was written correctly. If the reader thinks the evaluation is incomplete, it is the reader's responsibility to get a better explanation from the listener.

The written conferences may be taken from the room to further help the writers revise their rough drafts before the next day's conference.

The written evaluations must be turned in with the final copy in order for the writer to receive his 200 points. Conferences may be handed in for a grade before final copies are due. If this is done, they must still be included with the final copy. Getting the conferences early allows the teacher to spend all the grading time on the paper.

While the students conference with each other, conferences with the teacher are simultaneously held. These conferences last between three and five minutes and are not the same as the student-to-student conferences.

What Are Student-to-Teacher Conferences?

Teacher conferences are used to iron out problems that students are having with their papers. We have found that teachers do not have to ask the same questions that are asked during the student-to-student conferences. We use a variety of conference techniques. In some conferences we ask our students to briefly summarize their compositions. Sometimes we ask them to read a section of their paper that has good detail or emotion. Other times we will ask them to read us their opening or ending. Still other times we will just ask them if they have any questions for us about their papers.

From the student-to-teacher conference, the teacher becomes familiar with the paper's basic content, so while evaluating the paper, the teacher is free to concentrate on the aspects of the composition that the teacher feels are important.

For example, when evaluating expository compositions, we look for the elements that are on the students' lists and conference guidelines. These include the following items:

1. Strong introduction
2. One main idea per body paragraph
3. At least two supporting details for each main idea
4. A clincher sentence for each paragraph in the body
5. Transitions used between each body paragraph
6. Strong conclusion

After the conferencing is completed, the finishing touches should be made on the rough draft, and the students should begin working on the final copies.

Expository Conference Form

Title of Paper_____

Writer_____Conferrer_____

1. Did the introduction get your attention? Yes or No

   a. What did the introduction tell you?

2. Is there only one main idea in each paragraph?

   a. List the main ideas.

3. Are there enough supporting details for each main idea?

   a. If yes, list the supporting details in the best paragraph.

   b. If no, suggest some supporting details for a paragraph.

4. List all transitions used to connect paragraphs.

5. What is the most important idea in the composition?

6. Are there any technical terms used in the composition?

   a. If so, are they defined?

   b. If not, could any be added? If so, where?

7. Does the composition end with a strong impression? Yes or No

   a. If yes, what is the strong impression?

   b. If no, how could it become stronger?

CHAPTER NINETEEN

Expository Final Copies

A final copy is *not* the end product of the writing process. Rather, it is just a revised rough draft that is turned in as a required step of the process.

Like the other segments of the writing process, guidelines for writing a final copy must be established. Four things are required for final copies in our classes:

1. They must have a title.
2. They must be written in blue or black ink.
3. The writing can only be on one side of the paper.
4. Students must attach an opinion paragraph to the back of their compositions. The paragraph should tell how the student feels about the paper in terms of organization, detail, emotion, and flow of the overall paper.

The students, in addition to their final copy and opinion, must hand in their rough draft, two conferences, and list. These papers are all stapled together in the following order:

1. Final Copy
2. Opinion
3. Rough Draft
4. List
5. Two Conferences

Final copies are rated holistically rather than given a letter grade and are used as yet another form of feedback to the students.

CHAPTER TWENTY

Expository Holistic Scoring

In an earlier section we discussed making the students successful by awarding points in conjunction with holistic scoring. Now it is time to look at what holistic scoring is and how easy it is to use.

What Is Holistic Evaluation?

"With this method the evaluator is not concerned about specific traits in the writing or about particular criteria (though subconsciously the teacher may very well be working from an implicit primary trait checklist based on his or her own particular biases)"(Bechtel 1985: 171-172).

The holistic scoring of expository final copies provides the students with feedback about their work before it is turned in as a rewrite. It affords students the opportunity to focus on creating a strong composition they can revise later. Holistic scores have no bearing on the students' grades. It is not an "A," "B," "C," "D," or "F." It is just a general impression.

Holistic scales are designed for flexibility. Developing a scale that reflects individual teacher preferences is fairly easy to do. Our scale is a 0-6 rating scale, and it contains (in somewhat loose terms) our explanations of what we look for in students' expository papers. An example of our scale appears below:

6. Papers that are clearly excellent. The top score 6 is reserved for that paper clearly above a 5. The paper develops the story line with an interesting introduction and conclusion and supports the main ideas with strong detail. It also displays educated use of language and mechanics.

5. A thinner version of the excellent paper. It is still impressive, but not as well handled in terms of introduction, main ideas, supporting details, conclusion, language, and mechanics.

4. An above average paper. It has strong story line but may be deficient in one of the essentials mentioned above.

3. An average paper. It maintains a general story line and shows some sense of organization, but it is weak in its introduction, main ideas, supporting details, conclusion, language, and mechanics.

2. A below average paper. It maintains a general story line but demonstrates serious weaknesses in its introduction, main ideas, supporting details, conclusion, language, and mechanics. It is unacceptable for most standards.

1. A story line that has almost no redeeming quality. It may be brief or very long, but it will be scarcely coherent and full of mechanical errors as well.

0. A blank paper or an unacceptable effort.

Each student receives a copy of this holistic grading scale at the beginning of the year. It is used to evaluate all expository final copies. After writing one or two compositions, the students acquire a "feel" for the holistic scale. To help the students acquire this feel, we read strong examples to the class on the day that papers are returned, and point out why each paper received that score. We also read good segments of lower scoring papers that reflect strong detail and emotion but are deficient in other areas such as organization.

How Difficult Is Holistic Scoring?

The actual rating of the papers is reasonably simple and becomes easier with time. Evaluating a 300-500 word composition should only take between three and eight minutes, and that includes reading the paper and making comments about it.

How Can a Composition Be Evaluated in Three to Eight Minutes?

The teacher becomes familiar with the paper's general story line during the student-to-teacher conference. As a result, understanding the content is not cumbersome, and more time can be spent concentrating on the paper's organization (introduction, main ideas, supporting details, clincher sentences, transitions, and conclusion).

Should the Errors Be Marked?

We don't spend precious time marking mistakes found in the text. Research shows that students pay little attention to marks made within the text; they turn right to the end to find the final grade. Also when teachers mark errors students never learn to identify and correct their own weaknesses. We hope by not marking errors that the students will try to figure out the mistakes on their own or ask another student or us to help them. Those who do ask for assistance improve with time.

Where Do the Teachers' Comments Belong?

All of the comments regarding the paper's content, organization, emotion, and detail should be written at the end of the composition. Any grammar errors found in the story may also be noted.

Students quickly learn that the holistic score is based on their manipulation of several areas: the organization of ideas, the support of the main ideas, the flow of the story line, the use of detail, and the use of emotional language. As teachers come across papers they consider 5's or 6's, they should read them to their classes. After writing one or two compositions, students have a fairly good idea what the teacher considers a 0-6 paper. Once students are comfortable with holistic scoring, pluses and minuses and slashes can be used to give a more specific impression without making any comments. For example, a 4+ is more desirable than a 4-even though neither has any bearing on the students' grade. Likewise, a 3+ / 4- does not affect the overall grade, but it shows the students that some kind of progress has been made.

Even though holistic scoring requires some adjustment by both teachers and students, it will benefit both in the long run.

References

Bechtel, Judith. (1985). *Improving Writing and Learning*. Boston: Allyn and Bacon.

Expository Holistic Grading Scale

6 = Papers that are clearly excellent. The top score of 6 is reserved for that paper clearly above a 5. The paper develops the story line with an interesting introduction and conclusion and supports the main ideas with strong detail. It also displays educated use of language and mechanics.

5 = A thinner version of the excellent paper. It is still impressive, but not as well handled in terms of introduction, main ideas, supporting details, conclusion, language, and mechanics.

4 = An above average paper. It has strong story line but may be deficient in one of the essentials mentioned above.

3 = An average paper. It maintains a general story line and shows some sense of organization, but it is weak in its introduction, main ideas, supporting details, conclusion, language, and mechanics.

2 = A below average paper. It maintains a general story line but demonstrates serious weaknesses in its introduction, main ideas, supporting details, conclusion, language, and mechanics. It is unacceptable for most standards.

1 = A story line that has almost no redeeming quality. It may be brief or very long, but it will be scarcely coherent and full of mechanical errors as well.

0 = A blank paper or an unacceptable effort.

CHAPTER TWENTY-ONE

Grading Expository Rewrites

Near the end of each grading period, the students complete the last step of the writing process—the rewrite. The same basic guidelines that are used with creative rewrites apply to expository rewrites.

What Is the Purpose of Rewrites?

Students need the opportunity to experiment with their writing, and writing several compositions before they have to turn one in for a grade gives them that chance.

Through rewrites the students have the opportunity to further develop a final copy using the holistic grade as their guide.

How Do Rewrites Evolve?

First, a due date for the rewrite must be set. One week before the end of the grading period is a fair time.

Next, set a date for a one-day in-class rewrite conference. This should be three to five days before the rewrite is due.

Then, ask the students to choose their favorite final copy from the grading period to use for their rewrite. That final copy now becomes a rough draft, and the students should begin making changes on their compositions.

Most of the changes should be made prior to the scheduled conferencing day. This way the writer has something to gain from the new feedback that the conferencing provides.

This conferencing is student-to-student, and it is only necessary to require one conference. These conferences are not awarded any points; the "reward" for completing the conference is that the students are given a day in class to help improve a paper that counts as a major grade. The teacher should be accessible to the students if they need help, but teacher conferences are unnecessary when dealing with rewrites.

How Are Rewrites Graded?

Like creative rewrites, these rewrites also count as letter grades, and because the students have been given ample opportunity to improve their stories (first through the two student conferences, the teacher conference, the holistic grade, and finally through the rewrite conference) rewrites should also count as a weighted grade. A suggestion is to count the rewrite as 500 points (the same amount that the student accumulated while writing the paper for a final copy).

All of the aspects of the writing should be evaluated. This includes mechanics as well as introductions, topic sentences, supporting details, clinchers, and conclusions. The old final copy is handed in with the rewrite, so the teacher can see the changes made by the student.

How Much Time Is Spent Grading Rewrites?

Because the teacher has already been exposed to the basic content of the paper while grading it holistically, the time spent grading the rewrite should be minimal. Mistakes should be marked in the text as they are found, but it is unnecessary to correct them.

CHAPTER TWENTY-TWO

Creative and Expository Guided Writing Assignments

Often times, students are reluctant to jump right in and write a paper because they have not been successful in previous writing ventures. Other times, students are eager to write, but they lack direction. And still, there are those times when students want to write, have the ability to write, but they cannot make heads nor tails of the assignment.

How Do We Encourage Reluctant Writers?

When working with reluctant writers, we turn to guided writings. Guided writings provide the students with structure and at the same time they give them freedom to write what they want. Guided stories utilize process writing, but sometimes the steps are fused together in order to produce the final copy.

In this chapter we will walk through three of our guided writing activities and provide some step by step suggestions on how to use them. These papers rely heavily on process writing;

however, because of the desired outcome, some of the steps vary slightly from those previously explained throughout the book.

Guided Writing–Example One

The first example can be used with any group of students, but it works extremely well with writers who have cold feet. This guided activity will yield a six paragraph creative story that has a beginning, middle, and end. It can be divided several ways and will probably take three to five class periods to complete.

STEP ONE. This will be the S.W.A.P.ping activity, and it will take one day to complete. However, with this guided story, the S.W.A.P. will develop into the story. This step will also serve as the students' lists.

A. Find a picture of a lone character (perhaps a man on horseback), and show it to the students. The more vague the picture is the better. This will force students to use their imaginations. Based on what they see, ask them to answer all of the questions that appear below.

B. Provide students with the following list of questions:
    1. Who is the character?
    1. Describe the character?
        a. age
        b. height/weight
        c. hair/eye color
        d. clothing
        e. hobbies
        f. favorite food
        g. hometown

    2. What does the character do for a living?
    2. Where is the character going?
    2. Why?

    3. Why is the character being attacked?
    3. Who is attacking the character?
    3. Where is the character being attacked?

✍ This character is captured.

    4. Where is the character taken?
    4. What do the captors do to the character?
    4. How does the character escape?

5. How does the character feel about the escape?
5. Is this character injured?

6. Does the character get home safely?
6. Will the character make this trip again?
6. Is the character going to get revenge?

Note that there are sixteen questions arranged in six groups and one statement marked with an asterisk. The sentence about being captured must appear between the third and fourth group of questions.

C. Once the students have answered the questions, ask them to share their answers aloud with the class.

STEP TWO. Now the students will begin their rough drafts. This will take one to three class periods.

A. Tell the students to use the information from the questions numbered "one" to write a paragraph that describes their character.

B. Once the paragraph is completed, they should revise it. We suggest they use a modified version of our "Rough Draft Revision Checklist" that is discussed in Chapter Six.

Modified Creative Rough Draft Revision Checklist

1. Use strong verbs whenever possible.
   _____ Have I replaced weak verbs with strong action verbs wherever I could?
2. Use vivid detail and try to create a picture with words.
   _____ Are my explanations clear?
   _____ Have I created on paper the same images that I see in my mind?
3. Check for spelling errors.
   _____ Have I looked up in a dictionary words that I'm uncertain about?
   _____ Have I used **their/there/they're** and **your/you're** correctly?
4. Check for shifts in verb tense.
   _____ Do each of my paragraphs have consistent tense?

_____ Have I used the present perfect tense (placing **"has"** or **"have"** before the main verb) correctly?
a. Use it to show action that started in the past and is still going on in the present   **OR**
b. Use it to show action that happened at an indefinite time in the past.

_____ Have I used the past perfect tense (placing **"had"** before the main verb) correctly?
a. Use it when two actions have occurred in the past and one action was completed before the other.

5. Check for punctuation errors.

_____ Do I have punctuation marks at the ends of all my sentences?

_____ Are my commas in the right places?

_____ Have I used quotation marks correctly?

   C. Repeat steps A and B for each of the remaining five groups of questions. However, if the students can handle the work load, assign two or more paragraphs to write before they begin revising.

STEP THREE. Now the student should conference. This will take one class period.

   A. Put the students in groups of three. By conferencing in triads, the students will be able to complete both conferences during one class period.

   B. Give each student two blank conference sheets.

Creative Conference Form

Title of Story_____
Writer_____ Conferrer_____

   1. Was the beginning of the story interesting? Yes or No
     a. If it was, what made it interesting?
     b. If not, why wasn't it interesting?
   2. Was there any vivid detail used in the story? Yes or No
     a. Write the sentence that contains the best detail.
     b. Choose any sentence and add detail to it.
   3. Was there any emotion used in the story? Yes or No
     a. Write the sentence that contains the best emotion.

b. Choose any sentence and add emotion to it.

4. Write a brief summary of the story based on the following elements:

    a. Who?   (main character)

    b. What?   (main events in the story)

    c. Why?   (reasons the main events happened)

    d. When?   (time)

    e. Where?   (setting)

5. Did you like the ending of the story? Yes or No

    a. If you did, why did you like it?

    b. If you did not, what was wrong with it?

C. When the students finish conferencing, they should put the finishing touches on their rough drafts.

STEP FOUR. Now the students produce their final copies. This should take one day. We suggest giving the students a few options to choose from. Below are three examples:

A. CREATE A BOOK. Turn your story into a book. Create an original cover and identify yourself as the author. Give each paragraph its own page and illustrate it. Write a summary of your story on the back cover.

B. WRITE THE FINAL COPY IN TRADITIONAL FORM. Put the title in quotation marks on the top line. Write in blue or black ink, and write only on one side of the paper.

C. COMPLETE A WRAP UP SHEET. A "Wrap Up Sheet" is a great tool to use with younger or reluctant writers. We use "Wrap Up Sheets" in conjunction with reading the papers aloud. While the students read their papers out loud to the class, we follow along on the "Wrap Up Sheet." These sheets also help alleviate the grading paper load. Many times younger students' handwriting is atrocious, and it is tedious work for the teacher to read through an entire class of papers. Having heard the students' final copies, the teacher can skim the written pages and use the "Wrap Up Sheet" as a crutch while holistically evaluating the story.

Wrap-up Sheet

1. Title of your story:
2. Author:
3. Who is the main character?
4. What problem does the main character face?
5. How is the problem resolved?
6. How does the story end?
7. Write a section of your story that you think contains the best detail:
8. Write a section of your story that you think contains the best emotion:

Guided Writing–Example Two

The second example can also be used with any group of students. Like the first example, this activity works especially well with reluctant writers. When the students are finished with this guided story, they will have a five paragraph composition.

STEP ONE. This part of the activity will serve as the S.W.A.P.ping activity as well as the list.

A. First, students need to choose a survival topic. Some that they may opt for are as follows:
   - ✍ Surviving at scout camp
   - ✍ Surviving a baby-sitting job
   - ✍ Surviving in _____ class
B. Next, tell the students to list three things that could prevent survival in their chosen topic. For example, at scout camp, one obstacle might be the initiation of inexperienced campers. Or, while baby-sitting, one obstacle might be crying children.

   OBSTACLE ONE _____
   OBSTACLE TWO _____
   OBSTACLE THREE _____

C. Then, have the students suggest three ideas that could help them overcome each obstacle. They may choose to add some humorous methods that would aid survival. For example, "Crying children are a nuisance while baby-sitting. I suggest trying to be compassionate. Also, taking along some games and books for the kids to play with helps to pass the time. If all else fails, you can insert ear plugs to drown out the noise."

OBSTACLE ONE
1.
2.
3.
OBSTACLE TWO
1.
2.
3.
OBSTACLE THREE
1.
2.
3.

D. Ask the students to share aloud their obstacles to survival and also their methods for overcoming them.

STEP TWO. Show the students that they have completed the S.W.A.P. and list part of the writing process. Now they should write their rough drafts.

A. First, they should write a short paragraph (two or three sentences) that captures the audience's attention and also identifies the topic

B. Next, they should write a brief paragraph about each of the three obstacles. Within each paragraph they should describe the obstacle and offer their three suggestions for overcoming it.

C. Finally, they should write their conclusion. It should be two or three sentences expressing their opinion of the whole experience.

D. After the five paragraphs are written, the students should begin revising them. We suggest that they use a modified version of our "Rough Draft Revision Checklist" that is explained in Chapter Six.

Modified Creative Rough Draft Revision Checklist

1. Use strong verbs whenever possible.
_____   Have I replaced weak verbs with strong action verbs wherever I could?
2. Use vivid detail and try to create a picture with words.
_____   Are my explanations clear?

_____ Have I created on paper the same images that I see in my mind?

3. Check for spelling errors.

_____ Have I looked up in a dictionary words that I'm uncertain about?

_____ Have I used **their/there/they're** and **your/you're** correctly?

4. Check for shifts in verb tense.

_____ Do each of my paragraphs have consistent tense?

_____ Have I used the present perfect tense (placing **"has"** or **"have"** before the main verb) correctly?
a. Use it to show action that started in the past and is still going on in the present **OR**
b. Use it to show action that happened at an indefinite time in the past.

_____ Have I used the past perfect tense (placing **"had"** before the main verb) correctly?
a. Use it when two actions have occurred in the past and one action was completed before the other.

5. Check for punctuation errors.

_____ Do I have punctuation marks at the ends of all my sentences?

_____ Are my commas in the right places?

_____ Have I used quotation marks correctly?

STEP THREE. After the revisions are made, the students should conference.

A. Put the students in groups of three. By conferencing in triads, the students will be able to complete both conferences during one class period.

B. Give each students two blank conference sheets.

Creative Conference Form

Title of Story_____

Writer_____ Conferrer_____

1. Was the beginning of the story interesting? Yes or No
a. If it was, what made it interesting?
b. If not, why wasn't it interesting?

2. Was there any vivid detail used in the story? Yes or No
a. Write the sentence that contains the best detail.

  b. Choose any sentence and add detail to it.
3. Was there any emotion used in the story? Yes or No
  a. Write the sentence that contains the best emotion.
  b. Choose any sentence and add emotion to it.
4. Write a brief summary of the story based on the following elements:
  a. Who?　　　(main character)
  b. What?　　　(main events in the story)
  c. Why?　　　(reasons the main events happened)
  d. When?　　　(time)
  e. Where?　　(setting)
5. Did you like the ending of the story? Yes or No
  a. If you did, why did you like it?
  b. If you did not, what was wrong with it?

C.　When the students finish conferencing, they should put the finishing touches on their rough drafts.

STEP FOUR. Now it is time for the students to write their final copies. Give the students several options for completing their final copies. Some examples are listed below:

A.　CREATE A BOOK. Turn your story into a book. Create an original cover and identify yourself as the author. Give each paragraph its own page and illustrate it. Write a summary of your story on the back cover.

B.　WRITE THE FINAL COPY IN TRADITIONAL FORM. Put the title in quotation marks on the top line. Write in blue or black ink, and write only on one side of the paper.

C.　COMPLETE A WRAP UP SHEET. A "Wrap Up Sheet" is a great tool to use with younger writers. We use "Wrap Up Sheets" in conjunction with reading the papers aloud. While the students read their papers out loud to the class, we follow along on the "Wrap Up Sheet." These sheets also help alleviate the grading paper load. Many times younger students' handwriting is atrocious, and it is tedious work for the teacher to read through an entire class of papers. Having heard the students' final copies, the teacher can skim the written pages and use the "Wrap Up Sheet" as a crutch while holistically evaluating the story.

Wrap-up Sheet

1. Title of your story:
2. Author:
3. Who is the main character?
4. What problem does the main character face?
5. How is the problem resolved?
6. How does the story end?
7. Write a section of your story that you think contains the best detail:
8. Write a section of your story that you think contains the best emotion:

Guided Writing–Example Three

The third example is a guided expository composition and is best used with more mature writers. It is a persuasive writing that evolved from an assignment in a speech class.

Persuasive writing involves winning over the audience. The writers have to be convincing, and to accomplish this they must appeal to their audience's emotions and use logic when presenting the facts.

When we assign a persuasive composition, we are really telling our students, "Write a paper in which you ask your audience to change its beliefs." This is easier said than done, and it is also why this guided expository assignment came about.

The students will have written a five paragraph persuasive composition at the completion of this activity.

STEP ONE. Ask the students to choose a controversial topic and to describe the course of action that they want to take. It is important to have information available to students on the chosen topic.

A. The course of action should be a debatable subject.
B. It needs to be written in sentence form, and it also must contain the word "should."
C. Some samples appear below:
   1. High schools should increase the requirements for graduation.
   2. Females should have to register with the selective service.
D. Ask the students to share their ideas aloud and to give two reasons that they might use to support their course of action. This will serve as the S.W.A.P.ping activity.

STEP TWO. Now the students need time to gather and organize their information. We usually allow two class periods in the library for this.

STEP THREE. Once the students have organized their material, they need to make a list. This list is similar to the expository list described in Chapter Sixteen; the difference is that the students incorporate the purpose and introduction, they address specific points for the main ideas, and they tell the audience what to do in the conclusion.

A. Compare the list from Chapter Sixteen to the list for the persuasive guided writing.

Expository Lists	Persuasive Guided Writing
1. Topic	1. Topic
2. Purpose	2. Purpose
3. Audience	a. What problem exists?
4. Tone	b. What is your solution?
5. Title	3. Audience
6. Thesis	4. Tone
7. Main ideas	5. Title
8. Supporting details	6. Thesis
9. Transitions	7. Details of solution
10. Conclusion	8a. What is specific plan?
	8b. What are the rules?
	8c. Who will carry them out?
	7. Practicality of the plan
	8a. Has the idea worked in other places? If so, give examples.
	8b. Are any absolutes necessary to make the plan work?
	8c. Will this plan do what you claim it will?
	7. Benefits of plan for the audience
	8a.
	8b.
	8c.
	9. Transitions
	10.Conclusion—What can the audience do to help promote the plan?

STEP FOUR. After their lists are made, the students write their rough drafts. Once their rough drafts are completed, the students should revise them. We give them a modified expository "Rough Draft Revision Checklist" to use.

Modified Expository Rough Draft Revision Checklist

1. Underline topic sentences
_____ Have I underlined the topic sentence in each paragraph?
2. Put parentheses around the clincher sentences
_____ Have I put parentheses around each clincher sentence?
_____ Does each clincher sentence reflect the topic sentence?
3. Number each supporting detail–eliminate unnecessary details
_____ Have I numbered the supporting details?
_____ Are there at least two supporting details for each main idea?
_____ Have I crossed out the unnecessary details?
4. Circle all transitions used
_____ Have I circled all of the transitions?
_____ Did I use a transition between each paragraph in the body of the paper?
5. Check introduction and conclusion
_____ Is my introduction acceptable?
_____ Is my conclusion acceptable?
6. Check for shifts in verb tense
_____ Do each of my paragraphs have consistent tense?
_____ Have I used the present perfect tense (placing **"has"** or **"have"** before the main verb) correctly?
a. Use it to show action that started in the past and is still going on in the present
b. Use it to show action that happened at an indefinite time in the past.
_____ Have I used the past perfect tense (placing **"had"** before the main verb) correctly?
a. Use it when two actions have occurred in the past and one action was completed before the other.
7. Check for spelling errors
_____ Have I looked up in a dictionary words that I'm uncertain about?
_____ Have I used **their/there/they're** and **your/you're** correctly?

8. Check for punctuation errors

_____ Do I have punctuation marks at the ends of all my sentences?

_____ Are my commas in the right places?

_____ Have I used quotation marks correctly?

9. Use strong verbs when possible

_____ Have I replaced weak verbs with strong action verbs wherever I could?

10. Use vivid detail–try to create a picture with words

_____ Are my explanations clear?

_____ Have I created on paper the same images that I see in my mind?

STEP FIVE. When the revisions are made, the students should conference.

A. Put the students in groups of three. By conferencing in triads, the students will be able to complete both conferences during one period.

B. Give each student two blank conference sheets.

Expository Conference Form

Title of Story_____

Writer_____Conferrer_____

1. Did the introduction get your attention? Yes or No
   a. What did the introduction tell you?
2. Is there only one main idea in each paragraph?
   a. List the main ideas.
3. Are there enough supporting details for each main idea?
   a. If yes, list the supporting details in the best paragraph.
   b. If no, suggest some supporting details for a paragraph.
4. List all transitions used to connect paragraphs.
5. What is the most important idea in the composition?
6. Are there any technical terms used in the composition?
   a. If so, are they defined?
   b. If not, could any be added? If so, where?
7. Does the composition end with a strong impression? Yes or No
   a. If yes, what is the strong impression?
   b. If no, how could it become stronger?

STEP SIX. Finally, the students write their final copies. They should use the following guidelines:

A. Write only in blue or black ink.
B. Put the title in quotation marks and write it on the top line.
C. Write only on the front side of the paper.

Guided writings are gentle prods that can be used with reluctant writers. Raphael (1990: 398) provides a note of caution: "If used as traditional work sheets, handed out to be completed and then evaluated by the teacher, [guided writing assignments] can encourage more work sheet question-answer activities and even less composing and thinking about text."

Any writing assignment can be turned into a guided writing simply by building in structure in the areas that seem to need help. Teachers should make their own guided writing activities, so they can be individualized according to the needs of the students.

References

Raphael, Taffy E. (1990). "Writing and Reading: Partners in Constructing Meaning." *The Reading Teacher* February, 388-400.

Guided Writing–Example One Exercise

1. Who is the character?

1. Describe the character?
   a. age
   b. height/weight
   c. hair/eye color
   d. clothing
   e. hobbies
   f. favorite food
   g. hometown

2. What does the character do for a living?

2. Where is the character going?

2. Why?

3. Why is the character being attacked?

3. Who is attacking the character?

3. Where is the character being attacked?

& This character is captured.

4. Where is the character taken?

4. What do the captors do to the character?

4. How does the character escape?

5. How does the character feel about the escape?

5. Is this character injured?

6. Does the character get home safely?

6. Will the character make this trip again?

6. Is the character going to get revenge?

Modified Creative Rough Draft Revision Checklist

1. Use strong verbs whenever possible.

   _____ Have I replaced weak verbs with strong action verbs wherever I could?

2. Use vivid detail and try to create a picture with words.

   _____ Are my explanations clear?

   _____ Have I created on paper the same images that I see in my mind?

3. Check for spelling errors.

   _____ Have I looked up in a dictionary words that I'm uncertain about?

   _____ Have I used **their/there/they're** and **your/you're** correctly?

4. Check for shifts in verb tense.

   _____ Do each of my paragraphs have consistent tense?

   _____ Have I used the present perfect tense (placing **"has"** or **"have"** before the main verb) correctly?
   a. Use it to show action that started in the past and is still going on in the present **OR**
   b.Use it to show action that happened at an indefinite time in the past.

   _____ Have I used the past perfect tense (placing **"had"** before the main verb) correctly?
   a. Use it when two actions have occurred in the past and one action was completed before the other.

5. Check for punctuation errors.

   _____ Do I have punctuation marks at the ends of all my sentences?

   _____ Are my commas in the right places?

   _____ Have I used quotation marks correctly?

Creative Conference Form

Title of Story_____

Writer_____ Conferrer_____

1. Was the beginning of the story interesting? Yes or No
   a. If it was, what made it interesting?
   b. If not, why wasn't it interesting?

2. Was there any vivid detail used in the story? Yes or No
   a. Write the sentence that contains the best detail.
   b. Choose any sentence and add detail to it.

3. Was there any emotion used in the story? Yes or No
   a. Write the sentence that contains the best emotion.
   b. Choose any sentence and add emotion to it.

4. Write a brief summary of the story based on the following elements:
   a. Who?   (main character)
   b. What?   (main events in the story)
   c. Why?   (reasons the main events happened)
   d. When?   (time)
   e. Where?   (setting)

5. Did you like the ending of the story? Yes or No
   a. If you did, why did you like it?
   b. If you did not, what was wrong with it?

Wrap-up Sheet

1. Title of your story:

2. Author:

3. Who is the main character?

4. What problem does the main character face?

5. How is the problem resolved?

6. How does the story end?

7. Write a section of your story that you think contains the best detail:

8. Write a section of your story that you think contains the best emotion:

Guided Writing–Example Two Exercise

1.   Choose a survival topic. Some examples are listed below:

Surviving in _____ Class
Surviving Your First Job
Surviving a Baby-sitting Job
Surviving at Scout Camp
How to Survive _____

Topic chosen _____

2.   List three obstacles to survival in your chosen area. For example, at scout camp, one obstacle might be initiation of inexperienced campers. While baby-sitting, one obstacle might be crying children.

Obstacle One _____
Obstacle Two _____
Obstacle Three_____

3.   Devise three methods for overcoming each obstacle. You may include humorous methods also.

Obstacle One: Method One_____
               Method Two_____
               Method Three_____

Obstacle Two: Method One_____
               Method Two_____
               Method Three_____

Obstacle Three:Method One_____
               Method Two_____
               Method Three_____

4.   You have just completed your S.W.A.P. and made your list. In fact, you have almost written your whole story. Now all you have to do now is put it together and add a few finishing touches.

A. First, write a short paragraph (two or three sentences) that captures the audience's attention and also identifies your topic.

B. Next, write a brief paragraph about each of the three obstacles. Within each paragraph describe the obstacle and offer your three suggestions for overcoming it.

C. Finally, write your conclusion. It should be two or three sentences expressing your opinion of the whole experience.

D. After the five paragraphs are written, you should begin revising them. Use the modified "Rough Draft Revision Checklist."

5. Next, you need to conference.

6. After the conferences, begin your final copy.

Expository Guided Writing–Example Three Exercise

Persuasive Writing

1. Choose a controversial topic that demands some course of action as the topic of your paper.

2. Write your course of action as a "should" statement. For example, "High schools should tighten the requirements for graduation."

3. Go to the library and gather information about your topic.

4. Make your list. Use the modified expository list to help you.

5. Write your rough draft, and then begin revising it. There should be five paragraphs (an introduction, three body paragraphs that correspond with the three main ideas from your list, and a conclusion).

6. Conference after your rough draft is written. Make sure you have the expository conference sheet.

7. Add the finishing touches to your rough draft, and write the final copy.

Persuasive List–Guided Writing

1. Topic
2. Purpose
    a. What problem exists?
    b. What is your solution?
3. Audience
4. Tone
5. Title
6. Thesis
7. Details of solution
    8a. What is specific plan?
    8b. What are the rules?
    8c. Who will carry them out?
7. Practicality of the plan
    8a. Has the idea worked in other places? If so, give examples.
    8b. Are any absolutes necessary to make the plan work?
    8c. Will this plan do what you claim it will?
7. Benefits of plan for the audience
    8a.
    8b.
    8c.
9. Transitions
10. Conclusion—What can the audience do to help promote the plan?

Expository Rough Draft Revision Checklist

1. Underline topic sentences
   _____ Have I underlined the topic sentence in each paragraph?
2. Put parentheses around the clincher sentences
   _____ Have I put parentheses around each clincher sentence?
   _____ Does each clincher sentence reflect the topic sentence?
3. Number each supporting detail–eliminate unnecessary details
   _____ Have I numbered the supporting details?
   _____ Are there at least two supporting details for each main idea?
   _____ Have I crossed out the unnecessary details?
4. Circle all transitions used
   _____ Have I circled all of the transitions?
   _____ Did I use a transition between each paragraph in the body of the paper?
5. Check introduction and conclusion
   _____ Is my introduction acceptable?
   _____ Is my conclusion acceptable?
6. Check for shifts in verb tense
   _____ Do each of my paragraphs have consistent tense?
   _____ Have I used the present perfect tense (placing **"has"** or **"have"** before the main verb) correctly?
   a. Use it to show action that started in the past and is still going on in the present
   b. Use it to show action that happened at an indefinite time in the past.
   _____ Have I used the past perfect tense (placing **"had"** before the main verb) correctly?
   a. Use it when two actions have occurred in the past and one action was completed before the other.
7. Check for spelling errors
   _____ Have I looked up in a dictionary words that I'm uncertain about?
   _____ Have I used their/there/they're and your/you're correctly?
8. Check for punctuation errors
   _____ Do I have punctuation marks at the ends of all my sentences?
   _____ Are my commas in the right places?

_____ Have I used quotation marks correctly?

9. Use strong verbs when possible

_____ Have I replaced weak verbs with strong action verbs wherever I could?

10. Use vivid detail–try to create a picture with words

_____ Are my explanations clear?

_____ Have I created on paper the same images that I see in my mind?

Expository Conference Form

Title of Paper_____

Writer_____Conferrer_____

1. Did the introduction get your attention? Yes or No
   a. What did the introduction tell you?
2. Is there only one main idea in each paragraph?
   a. List the main ideas.
3. Are there enough supporting details for each main idea?
   a. If yes, list the supporting details in the best paragraph.
   b. If no, suggest some supporting details for a paragraph.
4. List all transitions used to connect paragraphs.
5. What is the most important idea in the composition?
6. Are there any technical terms used in the composition?
   a. If so, are they defined?
   b. If not, could any be added? If so, where?
7. Does the composition end with a strong impression? Yes or No
   a. If yes, what is the strong impression?
   b. If no, how could it become stronger?

CHAPTER TWENTY-THREE

Writing While Studying Literature

In our classes we teach both writing and literature. Our students read thirty-six to forty short stories or plays, fifteen to twenty-five poems, and two to four novels in addition to writing twelve to twenty compositions during the school year. Each literature unit lasts between two and four weeks. While on literature our students do not forget about writing. They are given writing assignments where they need to use detail, emotion, dialogue, persuasion, and factual information. They may have four to six small writing assignments during a two to four week literature unit.

What Is a Sample Literature Writing Assignment?

For example while studying *Macbeth* we ask our students to write a paragraph describing the outside of Macbeth's castle, Inverness.

The writing assignment can help the students better visualize the setting of the story and thus improve reading comprehension. They are taking something they know and are bringing it to the story. Now reading *Macbeth* is not just a passive act; there is interaction between readers and the story.

Even though it may not seem like much, it gives the students practice on writing detail and it gives them a clearer picture in their minds where the story is taking place.

These paragraphs are not difficult to grade because we are only looking for one thing, detail. We read through the paragraphs quickly, and depending on the efforts given, we assign a grade between zero and one hundred percent. Most of the time the detail is good and the grades are high. Again this fits with the philosophy of process writing. If a good effort is made, then the high grades will follow. Even though we do not grade anything except detail, we do expect strong detail and a solid effort.

This writing of the descriptive paragraphs could be an in class writing assignment or a homework assignment. Either way the paragraphs are not difficult to grade, and the students are practicing their detail.

These paragraphs written while studying literature are kept in the writing folders for future reference.

How Do We Use Literature Writings to Improve Compositions?

During student-to-teacher conferences we sometimes find places where their stories could use more detail, but for some reason the students do not see how they can add more detail. At this point we have them open their writing folders and locate the paragraph describing Macbeth's castle. If it is a good paragraph, we help them transfer those skills to their present composition. If the paragraph wasn't so good, we show them the similarities between the two efforts. Then we work to improve both, either verbally or in writing.

What Are Some Other Examples?

There are times when we combine emotion, dialogue, and persuasion in one writing assignment. While still studying *Macbeth*, we could have our students write an imaginary conversation between Banquo and his wife for the following situation: Banquo has just returned from battle and has to persuade his irate wife to let him go to Macbeth's castle for a party, and she is not invited to go along.

We explain to our students that we expect them to punctuate the dialogue correctly, show emotion, and be persuasive. They are to do this in a page or page and a half.

Again the papers are graded similarly to the descriptive paragraphs. Only now there are three areas to look for as we read.

Sometimes we have the students read these dialogues aloud for the entire class to hear. If we do this, we can possibly listen for the persuasion and emotion in each and make a note on a tablet. Then when we read the papers later, we only have to look for correct dialogue punctuation which saves valuable grading time.

Another writing assignment we have given our students is to have a famous living person meet up with one of the fictional characters just covered in literature. Then they can carry on a dialogue, ask questions of each other, compete against each other, or do anything the students wish them to do.

For example the President could meet the three witches in *Macbeth* who will predict his future. Some prior knowledge of the President or some brief research about his presidential policies might improve the types of questions asked of the witches. So now the students can mix facts and fiction when they write.

Reader response is the last example of writing while studying literature. In a paragraph we have our students respond to how they would have felt or acted if they were placed in a similar situation as the fictional character. Would they have reacted differently? Do they feel sorry for the character? Why or why not? Are they envious of the character? How would they help the character? What advice would they give the character?

These questions are just a starting point. The students can choose any angle they wish as long as they respond personally to some situation faced by a character in the story.

Reader response helps the students identify personally with what is happening on the printed page in front of them. They are linking themselves to the story. Hopefully, this too will improve reading comprehension.

An example would be the following situation: You are Malcolm, Duncan's son. Your father has just been murdered in Macbeth's castle. Would you have run away to England? Why or why not? What could be said to change Malcolm's mind or encourage him to go? How would you respond to this situation? Explain similarities and differences you would have.

Both creative and expository writing can be done while working on literature. It further gives the students a chance for success and at the same time they can practice on troublesome areas of writing.

Literature We Teach

British Literature, Twelfth Grade English
I.   Short stories, poems, and excerpts from novels
        "Beowulf"–translated by Burton Raffel
        "The Canterbury Tales"–translated by Nevill Coghill
        "Sir Gawain and the Green Knight"–translated by Burton
        Raffel
        "Morte d'Arthur"–Sir Thomas Malory
        "Paradise Lost"–John Milton
        "The Rime of the Ancient Mariner"–Samuel Taylor Coleridge
        "Pride and Prejudice"–Jane Austen
        "Ode to the West Wind"–Percy Bysshe Shelley
        "Ode on a Grecian Urn"–John Keats
        "Frankenstein"–Mary Shelley
        "Sir Patrick Spens"–Scottish Ballads
        "Bonnie George Campbell"–Scottish Ballads
        "Bonny Barbara Allan"–Scottish Ballads
        "Get Up and Bar the Door"–Scottish Ballads
        "My Last Duchess"–Robert Browning
        "The Secret Sharer"–Joseph Conrad
        "The Door in the Wall"–H.G. Wells
        "The Open Window"–Saki
        "The Verger"–Somerset Maugham
        "The Celestial Omnibus"–E. M. Forster
        "A Room of One's Own"–Virginia Woolf
        "Araby"–James Joyce
        "The Rocking Horse Winner"–D. H. Lawrence
        "Miss Brill"–Katherine Mansfield
        "Rapunzel, Rapunzel"–Jean Rhys
        "The Duke's Children"–Frank O'Connor
        A Portrait of an Artist as a Young Man–James Joyce
        "Shooting an Elephant"–George Orwell
        "Across the Bridge"–Graham Greene
        "Midnight's Children"–Salman Rushdie

II.   Novels and Plays
        Macbeth–Shakespeare
        The Importance of Being Earnest–Oscar Wilde
        Pygmalion–Bernard Shaw
        The Inferno–Dante
        One Flew Over the Cuckoo's Nest–Ken Kesey

American Literature, Eleventh Grade English

I.   Short stories, poems, and excerpts from novels
        "The Devil and Tom Walker"–Washington Irving
        "The Legend of Sleepy Hollow"–Washington Irving
        The Deerslayer–James Fennimore Cooper
        "The Fall of the House of Usher"–Edgar Allan Poe
        "The Masque of the Red Death"–Edgar Allan Poe
        "The Cask of Amontillado"–Edgar Allan Poe
        "The Raven"–Edgar Allan Poe
        "The Bells"–Edgar Allan Poe
        "Dr. Heidegger's Experiment"–Nathaniel Hawthorne
        "The Birthmark"–Nathaniel Hawthorne
        Typee–Herman Melville
        Moby Dick–Herman Melville
        "The Notorious Jumping Frog of Calaveras County"
                - Mark Twain
        "Baker's Bluejay Yarn"–Mark Twain
        "An Occurrence at Owl Creek Bridge"–Ambrose Bierce
        Life on the Mississippi–Mark Twain
        The Outcasts of Poker Flat–Bret Harte
        "The Open Boat"–Stephen Crane
        "The Sculptor's Funeral"–Willa Cather
        "To Build a Fire"–Jack London
        "Richard Cory"–Edwin Arlington Robinson
        "Miniver Cheevy"–Edwin Arlington Robinson
        "Mr. Flood's Party"–Edwin Arlington Robinson
        "George Gray"–Edgar Lee Masters
        "Lucinda Matlock"–Edgar Lee Masters
        "Fiddler Jones"–Edgar Lee Masters
        "Sophistication"–Sherwood Anderson
        "The Jilting of Granny Weatherall"–Katherine Anne Porter
        "The Catbird Seat"- James Thurber

"Winter Dreams"–F. Scott Fitzgerald
"The Bear"–William Faulkner
"The Devil and Daniel Webster" Stephen Vincent Benét
"Another April"–Jesse Stuart
"In Another Country"–Ernest Hemingway
"Flight"- John Steinbeck
"Lost"–Isaac Baschevis Singer
"A Worn Path"–Eudora Welty
"The First Seven Years"–Bernard Malamud
"The Life You Save May Be Your Own"–Flannery O'Connor
"The Lucid Eye in Silver Town"–John Updike
"Everyday Use"–Alice Walker

II.   Novels and Plays
Trifles–Susan Glaspell
Our Town–Thorton Wilder
The Glass Menagerie–Tennessee Williams
Cat on a Hot Tin Roof–Tennessee Williams
Cannery Row–John Steinbeck
Daisy Miller–Henry James
The Scarlet Letter–Nathaniel Hawthorne

CHAPTER TWENTY-FOUR

Lesson Plans and Time Tables

Quite often as teachers we teach the same class three different periods during the day. We, like many teachers, prefer to keep our classes all working on about the same lesson.

How Can Teachers Handle the Paper Load if Three Classes Start a Writing Unit at the Same Time?

Below, a chart shows how teachers can handle the paper load of three English classes writing at the same time. This chart gives examples of two compositions being written in a row, after which a literature unit is started.

The final copies for each class are never due at the same time. This way teachers will only ever have one class of papers to grade on a given day. With our holistic scoring system and with practice using it, even a class of thirty-two students can be graded in less than two and a half hours. That time is based on spending five minutes per paper. As teachers become more comfortable with the holistic scale, the time spent on each paper will decrease to around three minutes per paper. This computes to less than an hour and forty minutes.

These samples have been taken directly from our lesson plans, so we have extensively tested them.

The chart may seem confusing at first, but this chart merely represents what parts of process writing we are covering on a particular day. It is not a lesson plan. Sample lesson plans for the first week of English IV Period 1 appear later in this chapter.

Eng. IV Period 1	Eng. IV Period 3	Eng. IV Period 4
Monday Return final copy Start SWAP Assign: None	Monday Finish conferencing Start final Assign: Do final copy	Monday Continue conferencing Assign: Revise RD
Tuesday Finish SWAP Start list Assign: Do List	Tuesday Collect final copy SWAP Assign: Do list	Tuesday Finish conferencing Start final copy Assign: Do final copy
Wednesday Check list Start RD Assign: Do first three paragraphs of Rough Draft	Wednesday Check list Start Rough Draft Assign: Do Rough Draft	Wednesday Collect final Start SWAP Assign: None
Thursday Check first three paragraphs of RD Finish RD Assign: Finish RD	Thursday Check Rough Draft Start conferencing Assign: Revise RD	Thursday Return final copy Finish SWAP Assign: Do list
Friday Check Rough Draft Start conferencing Assign: Revise RD	Friday Continue conferencing Assign: Revise RD	Friday Check list Start RD Assign: Do RD

Eng. IV Period 1	Eng. IV Period 3	Eng. IV Period 4
Monday Continue conferencing draft Assign: Revise RD	Monday Finish conferencing Start final copy Assign: Do final copy	Monday Check rough Start conferencing Assign: Revise RD
Tuesday Finish conferencing Start final copy Assign: Do final copy	Tuesday Collect final copy Discuss final copies Intro to lit. unit Assign: Start lit.	Tuesday Continue conferencing Assign: Revise RD
Wednesday Collect final copy Intro to lit. unit Assign: Start lit.	Wednesday Return final copy Start grammar lesson Assign: Do Continue lit.	Wednesday Finish conferencing Start final copy Assign: Do final copy
Thursday Return final copy Start grammar lesson Assign: Continue lit.	Thursday Discuss lit. Continue grammar Assign: Continue lit.	Thursday Collect final copy Intro. to lit. Assign: Start lit.
Friday Discuss lit. Assign: Continue lit.	Friday Discuss lit. Assign: Continue lit.	Friday Return final copy Start grammar Assign: Continue lit.

The suggestions on these charts are just that, suggestions. The length of time spent on S.W.A.P.ping, or writing the rough draft, or conferencing will vary. The size of the classes, the personalities of the classes, or even the ever changing daily schedules of the teachers help determine the length of time spent on each composition.

We have spent as few as five class days working on a composition. We have also spent up to eight classes to get a final copy turned in. There is no length of time that works all the time for everyone. By changing the writing schedules, we do not fall into a rut. This flexible schedule also helps keep the students from getting bored with the steps of process writing.

What follows next are actual lesson plans for teaching process writing. These lesson plans cover five days and clearly state materials, objectives, procedures, and evaluation.

Day One

Length of Activity: One class period

Materials: S.W.A.P.ping activity, paper, pens

Objectives: 1. Students will practice writing in their journals.

2. Students will use all of the language arts skills (reading, writing, speaking, listening) to help them choose a topic for writing.

Procedure: I. (5 min.) Students write journal entries

II. (40 min. total) S.W.A.P.ping Activity— "Magic Potion"

A. (3-5 min.) Place a bottle of brightly colored liquid in front of the class

B. Tell them it is a magic potion, and ask them to briefly answer the following questions:

1. What is this potion called?

2. When is it used?

3. What happens when it is used?

4. What would happen if the bottle were accidentally knocked off the table and the potion spilled?

5. Describe the specific results.

C. (5 min.) Have students write a paragraph that incorporates their answers

D. (30 min.) Ask students to share their creations aloud

III. Assignment: Think of some ideas for your story

Evaluation: The S.W.A.P.ping Activity is used to help the students generate ideas for a story

Day Two

Length of Activity: One class period

Materials: paper, pens, items to be put in the lists

Objectives: 1. Students will practice writing in their journals

                2. Students will use all of the language arts skills as they share their ideas and begin writing their lists

Procedure: I. (5 min.) Students write journal entries

           II. (20-35 min.) Have students share their story ideas

           III. (10 min.) Students begin writing their lists
Make sure that students have the list of items
1. Who are the characters in your story?
2. What are your characters like?
   a. age
   b. height/weight
   c. hair/eye color
   d. clothing
   e. hobbies
   f. favorite food
   g. hometown
3. Where does your story take place?
   a. town
   b. state
   c. specific building
4. What time does your story take place?
   a. morning, afternoon, evening
   b. past, present, future
5. What problem or problems are your characters going to face?
6. What will they do to resolve the problem?
7. How will the story end?

          IV. Assignment: Finish writing lists

Evaluation: From the additional sharing of ideas, the students should be well on their way to completing their lists

Day Three

Length of Activity: One class period

Materials: students' lists, paper, pens, rough draft revision check lists

Objectives: 1. Students will practice writing in their journals

2. Students will continue to practice their writing skills while writing their rough drafts

Procedure: I. (5 min.) Students write journal entries—grade, record, and return lists while they write

II. Make sure students have rough draft revision checklist
1. Use strong verbs whenever possible
2. Use vivid detail to create a picture with words
3. Divide the story into paragraphs
4. Check for spelling errors
5. Check for shifts in verb tense
6. Check for punctuation errors

III. (40 min.) Students write their rough drafts and begin revisions

IV. Assignment: Continue revisions and be ready to conference

Evaluation: After reviewing the rough draft revision checklist, the students should be able to complete their homework assignment with little trouble

Day Four

Length of Activity: One class period (possibly part of next day)

Materials: students' revised rough drafts, paper, pens, list of the conferencing guidelines

Objectives: 1. Students will practice writing in their journals

2. Students will use all of the language arts skills while revising and conferencing

Procedure: I.   (5 min.) Students write in journals—grade, record, and return rough drafts while they write

II. Make sure that students have conference guidelines
   1.   Was the beginning of the story interesting? Y or N
        If it was, what made it interesting?
        If not, why wasn't it interesting?
   2.   Was there any vivid detail used in the story? Y or N
        Write the sentence that contains the best detail.
        Choose any sentence and add detail to it.
   3.   Was there any emotion used in the story? Y or N
        Write the sentence that contains the best emotion.
        Choose any sentence and add emotion to it.
   4.   Write a brief summary of the story based on the following elements:
             Who?
             What?
             Why?
             When?
             Where?
   5.   Did you like the ending of the story? Y or N
        If you did, why did you like it?
        If you did not, what was wrong with it?

III. (40 min.) Student to student conferences (each student must have two conferences to turn in with the final copy)
student to teacher conferences are simultaneously held

IV. Assignment: Continue making revisions to the rough drafts

Evaluation: The conferences give the students a chance to get immediate feedback about their stories and also provide an audience

Day Five

Length of Activity: One class period

Materials: students' revised rough drafts and all other steps of the writing process (list, conferences), pens paper

Objectives: 1. Students will practice writing in their journals

2. Students will continue improving their writing skills while completing their final copies

Procedure: I. (5 min.) Students write journal entries

II. (40 min.) Students write their final copies. Students may also use this time to complete last minute conferencing details, but they must turn in their final copies at the end of the period.

Final copies should be written in blue or black ink; they must have a title in quotation marks at the top of the page; writing should be only on one side of the paper; there must be an opinion paragraph attached at the end of the final copy.

Evaluation: By following all the steps of the writing process, the students should have produced their best possible effort on this paper.

Our writing program is designed for flexibility as is demonstrated by the previous chart; however, teachers can adhere to a straight schedule and keep the students in every class at the same pace if they wish.

Completing a Composition in Five, Six, or Seven Days

Writing can take five to seven class days per composition, and keeping students at the same pace can be accomplished by using the guidelines in the following time tables.

The first table sets up a five day composition. It gives the students the weekend to complete the final copies.

Time Table # 1

DAY	WORK IN CLASS	ASSIGNMENT
Monday	S.W.A.P in class	List due for Tuesday
Tuesday	Check lists Start rough drafts	Finish rough drafts
Wednesday	Check rough drafts Start conferencing	Work on rough drafts
Thursday	Continue conferencing	Work on rough drafts
Friday	Finish conferencing Start final copy	Final copy due Monday

The second table requires six days to produce a final copy.

Time Table #2

DAY	WORK IN CLASS	ASSIGNMENT
Monday	S.W.A.P in class	None
Tuesday	Finish S.W.A.P. Start list	Lists due Wednesday
Wednesday	Check lists Start rough drafts	Finish rough drafts
Thursday	Check rough drafts Start conferencing	Work on rough drafts
Friday	Continue conferencing	Work on rough drafts
Monday	Finish conferencing Start final copy	Final copy due Tuesday

The third table takes seven days to produce a final copy.

Time Table # 3

DAY	WORK IN CLASS	ASSIGNMENT
Monday	Start S.W.A.P in class	None
Tuesday	Finish S.W.A.P. Start lists	Lists due
Wednesday	Check lists Start rough drafts	First half of rough drafts due Thursday
Thursday	Work on rough drafts	Finish rough drafts
Friday	Check rough drafts Start conferencing	Work on rough drafts
Monday	Continue conferencing	Work on rough drafts
Tuesday	Finish conferencing Start final copy	Final copy due Wednesday

What Do We Expect Our Students to Gain from This Holistic Approach to the Writing Process?

Donald Murray says it best for us, "I cannot tell what my students will be asked to do in their many disciplines, and I certainly cannot tell what they will be asked to write in the years after they leave school. Therefore, I try to teach my students a writing process or, better yet, have them develop their own process of writing they will be able to apply to the tasks that lie ahead of them" (Murray 1985: 239).

References

Murray, Donald.(1985). *A Writer Teaches Writing*. Boston: Houghton Mifflin Company.

CHAPTER TWENTY-FIVE

U.S. Department of Education Recommendations

In 1986 the United States Department of Education together with William J. Bennett, Secretary published the pamphlet *What Works: Research About Teaching and Learning*. In it are listed research findings and comments on many areas concerning education today. One of the research areas was Teaching Writing. The following is the research finding of the U.S. Department of Education: "The most effective way to teach writing is to teach it as a process of brainstorming, composing, revising, and editing" (27). This coincides with the program of writing that our students follow.

In addition to the research finding the following comments were made:

> Students learn to write well through frequent practice. A well-structured assignment has a meaningful topic, a clear sense of purpose, and a real audience. Good writing assignments are often an extension of class reading, discussion, and activities; not isolated exercises.

> An effective writing lesson contains these elements:

✍ **Brainstorming**: Students think and talk about their topics. They collect information and ideas, frequently much more than they will finally use. They sort through their ideas to organize and clarify what they want to say.

✍ **Composing**: Students compose a first draft. This part is typically time consuming and hard, even for very good writers.

✍ **Revising**: Students re-read what they have written, sometimes collecting responses from teachers, classmates, parents, and others. The most useful teacher response to an early draft focuses on what students are trying to say, not the mechanics of writing. Teachers can help most by asking for clarification, commenting on vivid expressions or fresh ideas, and suggesting ways to support the main thrust of writing. Students can consider the feedback and decide how to use it to improve the next draft.

✍ **Editing**: Students then need to check their final version for spelling, grammar, punctuation, other writing mechanics, and legibility.

Prompt feedback from teachers on written assignments is important. Students are most likely to write competently when schools routinely require writing in all subject areas, not just in English class (27).

In our process S.W.A.P.ping and listing are comparable to **Brainstorming**; for us **Composing** is writing a rough draft; **Revising** and **Editing** are similar to our rough draft revision checklist and conferencing guidelines.

Also noted is prompt feedback, and our holistic grading system provides for that immediate feedback.

Below are listed all of the references used to compile the research findings and comments for the U.S. Department of Education:

Elbow, P. (1981). *Writing With Power: Techniques for Mastering the Writing Process*. New York: Oxford University Press.

Emig, J. (1971). *The Composing Processes of Twelfth Graders*. Urbana, IL: National Council of Teachers of English. NCTE Research Rep. No. 13. ERIC Document No. ED 058205.

Graves, D.H. (1978). *Balancing the Basics: Let Them Write.* New York: The Ford Foundation. ERIC Document No. ED 192364.

Graves, D.H. (1983). *Writing: Teachers and Children at Work.* Exeter, NH: Heinemann.

Hillcocks, G., Jr. (November 1984). "What Works in Teaching Composition: A Meta-Analysis of Experimental Treatment Studies." *American Journal of Education*, Vol. 93, No. 1, pp. 133-170.

Humes, A. (1981). *The Composing Process: A Summary of the Research.* Austin, TX: Southwest Regional Laboratory. ERIC Document No. ED 222925.

The U.S. Department of Education pamphlet, *What Works: Research About Teaching and Learning* also researched Direct Instruction and disclosed the following research finding: "When teachers explain exactly what students are expected to learn, and demonstrate the steps needed to accomplish a particular academic task, students learn more" (35).

We feel this is excellent support for the organized, structured steps we use in our process.

The comments issued by the Department of Education reflect our philosophy of giving the students attainable goals and an opportunity to succeed simply by completing each step of our process.

Below are the comments:

The procedure stated above is called "direct instruction." It is based on the assumption that knowing how to learn may not come naturally to all students, especially to beginning and low-ability learners. Direct instruction takes children through learning steps systematically, helping them see both the purpose and the result of each step. In this way, children learn not only a lesson's content but also a method for learning that content.

The basic components of direct instruction are:
✍ setting clear goals for students and making sure they understand those goals,
✍ presenting a sequence of well-organized assignments,
✍ giving students clear, concise explanations and illustrations of the subject matter,

✍ asking frequent questions to see if children understand the work, and

✍ giving students frequent opportunities to practice what they have learned.

Direct instruction does not mean repetition. It does mean leading students through a process and teaching them to use that process as a skill to master other academic tasks. Direct instruction has been particularly effective in teaching basic skills to young and disadvantaged children, as well as in helping older and higher ability students to master more complex materials and to develop independent study skills (35).

The following references were used to determine the research findings and comments on Direct Instruction:

Berliner, D., and Rosenshine, B. (1976). *The Acquisition of Knowledge in the Classroom.* San Francisco: Far West Laboratory for Educational Research and Development.

Doyle, W. (1985). "Effective Secondary Classroom Practices." In R.M.J. Kyle (Ed.), *Researching for Excellence: An Effective Schools Sourcebook.* Washington, D.C.: U.S. Government Printing Office.

Good, T. and Grouws, D. (1981) *Experimental Research in Secondary Mathematics Classrooms: Working with Teachers.* Columbia, MO: University of Missouri.

Hansen, J. (1981). "The Effects of Inference Training and Practice on Young Children's Reading Comprehension." *Reading Research Quarterly*, Vol. 16, No. 3, pp. 391-417.

Rosenshine, B. (1983). "Teaching Functions in Instructional Programs." *Elementary School Journal*, Vol. 83, No. 4, pp. 335-351.

If the U.S. Department of Education feels that process writing is important, why aren't all teachers using it? We feel it is because a clear step by step explanation for implementing process writing is not available to all teachers. This book *The Pen Is In My Hand* . . . provides those clear step by step instructions.

References

U.S. Department of Education. (1986). *What Works: Research About Teaching and Learning.* Washington D.C.: U.S. Government Printing Office.

BIBLIOGRAPHY

Armbruster, B. and T. Anderson. (1982). "Idea Mapping: The Technique and Its Use in the Classroom." **Reading Educator Report.** No. 36. Urbana, Illinois: Center for the Study of Reading.

Bechtel, Judith. (1985). **Improving Writing and Learning.** Boston: Allyn and Bacon.

Berliner, D., and Rosenshine, B. (1976). **The Acquisition of Knowledge in the Classroom.** San Francisco: Far West Laboratory for Educational Research and Development.

Daigon, A. (1982). "Toward Righting Writing." **Phi Delta Kappa.** December, 242-246.

Doyle, W. (1985). "Effective Secondary Classroom Practices." In R.M.J. Kyle (Ed.), **Researching for Excellence: An Effective Schools Sourcebook.** Washington, D.C.: U.S. Government Printing Office.

Elbow, P. (1981). **Writing With Power: Techniques for Mastering the Writing Process.** New York: Oxford University Press.

Emig, J. (1971). **The Composing Processes of Twelfth Graders.** Urbana, IL: National Council of Teachers of English. NCTE Research Rep. No. 13. ERIC Document No. ED 058205.

Farr, Roger. (1990). "Reading Trends." **Educational Leadership.** November, 103.

Good, T. and Grouws, D. (1981) **Experimental Research in Secondary Mathematics Classrooms: Working with Teachers.** Columbia, MO: University of Missouri.

Graves, D.H. (1978). **Balancing the Basics: Let Them Write.** New York: The Ford Foundation. ERIC Document No. ED 192364.

---. (1983). ***Writing: Teachers and Children at Work.*** Exeter, New Hampshire: Heinemann.

Haley-James, S. (1981). ***Perspectives on Writing in Grades 1–8.*** Urbana, Illinois: National Council of Teachers of English.

Hansen, J. (1981). "The Effects of Inference Training and Practice on Young Children's Reading Comprehension." ***Reading Research Quarterly***, Vol. 16, No. 3, pp. 391-417.

---. (1992). "Literacy Portfolios Emerge." ***The Reading Teacher.*** April, 604-607.

Harp, B. (1988). "When the Principal Asks." ***The Reading Teacher.*** April, 828-830.

Hartwell, P. (1985). "Grammar, Grammars, and the Teaching of Grammar." ***College English.*** February, 105-27.

Hillcocks, G., Jr. (November 1984). "What Works in Teaching Composition: A Meta-Analysis of Experimental Treatment Studies." ***American Journal of Education***. Vol. 93, No. 1, pp. 133-170.

Humes, A. (1981). ***The Composing Process: A Summary of the Research.*** Austin, TX: Southwest Regional Laboratory. ERIC Document No. ED 222925.

Murray, Donald M. (1985). ***A Writer Teaches Writing.*** Boston: Houghton Mifflin Company.

Parker, J.F. (1991). ***Writing Process to Product.*** Evanston, Illinois: McDougal, Littell & Company.

Raphael, Taffy E., Carol Sue Englert. (1990). "Writing and Reading: Partners in Constructing Meaning." ***The Reading Teacher*** February, 388-400.

Raphael, Taffy E., Becky W. Kirschner, Carol Sue Englert. (1988). "Expository Writing Program: Making Connections Between Reading and Writing." ***The Reading Teacher*** April, 790-795.

Rosenshine, B. (1983). "Teaching Functions in Instructional Programs." *Elementary School Journal*, Vol. 83, No. 4, pp. 335-351.

Schwartz, Mimi. (1985). *Writing for Many Roles.* New Jersey: Boynton/Cook Publishers, Inc.

Simmons, John S. (1989). "Thematic Units: A Context for Journal Writing." *English Journal.* January, 70-72.

U.S. Department of Education. (1986). *What Works: Research About Teaching and Learning.* Washington D.C.: U.S. Government Printing Office.

Weeks, J.O. & M. White. (1982). *Peer Editing Versus Teacher Editing: Does It Make a Difference?* [ERIC ED 224 014].

Wiener, Harvey S. (1981). *The Writing Room.* New York: Oxford University Press.

Woodman, L. (1975). *Creative Editing: An Approach to Peer Criticism.* [ERIC ED 116 217].

GLOSSARY

audience –   the people who will listen to or read a composition

clincher sentence – usually the last sentence of a paragraph that restates the topic sentence in different words

composition -   a paper written to complete a writing assignment – a final copy–a rewrite–a writing–a story

conclusion -   the last paragraph of an expository composition

conference -   people taking turns reading, listening to, and evaluating a composition according to specific process writing guidelines

conferences -   the written evaluations of the listener turned in to the teacher so the reader can receive a grade on it

conferencing -   the act of people reading, listening to, and evaluating a composition

creative writing–   compositions that have a beginning, middle, end, strong detail, and strong emotion; but lack the formal structure of topic sentences, supporting details for each topic sentence, and a clincher associated with every paragraph of expository writing

expository writing- compositions that have a beginning, middle, end, detail, and emotion; but for every paragraph of the body of the composition there is a topic sentence, at least two supporting details for each topic sentence, and a clincher sentence

final copy -   the paper handed in that follows the conferencing step of process writing—it is written in blue or black ink on one side of the paper or typed double spaced–it is also holistically graded

final product - a paper written to complete a writing assignment–a final copy–a rewrite–a writing–a story

holistic grade - a number 0–6 that reflects from the teacher's overall impression of a piece of writing–it does not represent a letter grade or a percentage grade

holistic grading scale - the format used to evaluate a final copy that is nothing more than the teacher's general impression of a final copy

holistic scoring - the act of putting a general impression score on a paper

journal - the writing done the first five minutes of every class–it contains a title, the time started, the time finished, five minutes of effort, and an entry into the table of contents–these are saved for the entire school year

journal project - the culminating work done with the daily journals–it involves gathering together all of the daily journals for a year–organizing them–making a chart–and writing a composition that discusses all or part of the student's year in school–completely explained in Chapter Nine

list - the information a student thinks they might want to put into a composition–creative and expository lists differ as far as their content

listener - the person during conferencing who listens to the reader, and then writes up a conference for the reader main idea - the important point found in each topic sentence of expository compositions

paper - composition–piece of writing–final copy - rewrite–a writing–a story

portfolio - a folder that keeps an organized accumulation of different kinds of papers that reflect the students best efforts

process writing - steps that are followed in order to produce a final product - those steps are: S.W.A.P.ping, making a list, writing a rough draft, conferencing, and producing a final copy

purpose - is the aim of the composition–it could be to persuade, inform, convince, describe, explain, entertain, complain, etc.

rewrite - one of the old final copies that has been worked on some more and turned in at the end of a grading quarter for a percentage

rough draft - the initial writing of a composition that is done without regard to spelling, grammar, or punctuation–the ideas are written down quickly so they are not forgotten–once written it is then revised

S.W.A.P.ping Activity - Any whole class writing assignment written and shared in class with the purpose of generating possible writing topics for students

story line - the plot of a composition

story - a composition –a piece of writing–a paper - a final copy–a rewrite–a writing

strong verbs - verbs that give life to a piece of writing

supporting details - information that reinforces a topic sentence

thesis -

a sentence or a paragraph that states the purpose of a piece of expository writing

title -

reflects the content or purpose of a piece of writing

tone -

the mood of a certain composition

topic sentence -

the sentence that contains the main idea of a paragraph

topic -

the central focus of a paper

traditional brainstorming -

a technique used to develop an idea into a story

transitions -

words used to link ideas within a paragraph or between paragraphs

vivid detail -

words used to paint a picture with words

writers' voice–

the ability of writers to get the readers to share with them their emotions, opinions, struggles, and victories

writing folder -

a folder where students keep all types of writings done during a school year–this includes S.W.A.P.s, lists rough drafts, final copies, rewrites, writings done while studying literature, and possibly even journals - some papers are unfinished or in a rough draft form

writing process -

steps that are followed in order to produce a final product–those steps are: S.W.A.P.ping, making a list, writing a rough draft, conferencing, and producing a final copy

AUTHOR INDEX

ABOUT THE AUTHORS

Laura and I are presently teaching at Tuscarawas Valley Jr.-Sr. High School located in scenic Zoarville, Ohio. Our high school has around 750 students in grades 7—12. Tuscarawas Valley is a rural school with a wide socio-economic range.

Our teaching day starts at 7:30 A.M. and ends at 3:00 P.M. Laura teaches three classes of college prep junior English, one class of honors junior English, one class of speech, and two classes of seventh grade reading during a nine period day.

I teach three classes of college prep senior English, one class of honors senior English, one class of advanced writing, and one class of high school remedial reading. Each of our class periods is forty-five minutes long.

We see between 150—170 students each day. In addition to our teaching schedule we both have a lunch period and one conference/resource period. Instead of seven classes like Laura, I monitor a study hall of 150 students to complete my nine period day.

Laura has been teaching seven years, and all seven years have been at Tuscarawas Valley.

I have been teaching eighteen years but only the last five at Tuscarawas Valley. Right out of Defiance College I took a job at Tinora High School near Defiance, Ohio, where I spent eight years. From there I moved on to Newcomerstown High School in Newcomerstown, Ohio, for five years before settling in at Tuscarawas Valley.

Laura has her undergraduate and Masters Degree in Education from the University of Akron, and I have my Masters Degree in Education as a Reading Specialist from Kent State University.

As a change of pace from high school, we also teach part-time for Kent State University at the Tuscarawas Branch Campus located in New Philadelphia, Ohio. There Laura teaches the first two levels of freshman composition. I teach two different reading and study skills classes and the introductory freshman composition class. Here we see between 30—50 students two nights per week.

All of our classes, whether they are high school or college, remedial or honors learn process writing. This is the eleventh year I have worked with process writing. Nine of those years I consider successful years. My first two years of work were difficult, because I had to organize many ideas into my teaching style and change my old ways. After hours of reading and talking with high school teachers and college professors, I put together this writing process found in *The Pen Is in My Hand* . . .

Laura and I have been working together for only three years refining this process and putting it into our book. Even though it is basically the same process I started with eleven years ago, it is now better defined and explained .

When we are not teaching high school or college students or writing a book or magazine articles, we are making presentations at local, state, and national English and reading conventions. During the school year we also conduct inservice workshops for teachers in grades K - 12+ on all phases of process writing.

We hope everyone will enjoy *The Pen Is in My Hand* . . . as much as we enjoyed putting it together.

Jim Lindon
Laura Raber

GET MORE BOOKS FROM R & E AND SAVE!

TITLES	ORDER #	PRICE
The Pen is in My Hand...Now What?		
Exciting and Practical Ideas for Teaching Writing	048-X	$11.95
Towards a Thinking Curriculum		
Making Right Behavior Part of our Society	854-0	10.95
How the Universe Was Born		
The Big-Bang Concept Buried!	858-3	11.95
For Teachers Only:		
Personal and Confidential	889-3	9.95
Play on Words: Klever Word Puzzles for Very Klever People		
A Fast Laugh—With Quick Wit Word Puzzles	969-5	9.95
Revenge in the Classroom: Skool Kartoons for Everyone		
You'll Love to Laugh and Share the Humor of Education!	966-0	$9.95
The Presentation Handbook:		
How To Prepare Dynamic and Non-Technical Presentations		
What Makes a Good Instructor and How To Become One	872-9	14.95
Statistics In Science		
A Student's and Teacher's Manual For Science,		
Math & Computer Science Projects & Experiments	903-9	14.95

ORDER ANY 4 TITLES & GET ONE FREE—PLUS FREE POSTAGE!

Please rush me the following books. I want to save by ordering four books and receive a free book plus free postage. Orders under four books please include $3.00 shipping. CA residents add 8.25% tax.

YOUR ORDER

ORDER #	QUANTITY	UNIT PRICE	TOTAL PRICE

PAYMENT METHOD

☐ Enclosed Check or Money Order

☐ Master Card

☐ Visa

Card Expires —————

Signature —————

RUSH SHIPMENT TO:

(Please print)

Name —————

Organization —————

Address —————

City/State/Zip —————

R & E Publishers ● P.O. Box 2008 ● Saratoga, CA 95070
● (408) 866-6303 ● FAX (408) 866-0825